AN UNRECORDED CHAPTER

OF THE

INDIAN MUTINY

AN UNRECORDED CHAPTER

OF THE

INDIAN MUTINY.

BEING THE PERSONAL REMINISCENCES OF

REGINALD G. WILBERFORCE

GYAN

Published by

GYAN

Gyan Publishing House
5, Ansari Road
Daryaganj, New Delhi-110002
Phone: 011-47034999, 9811692060
E-mail: books@gyanbooks.com

Distribution Network
gyanbooks.com
India, USA, Canada, UK, Australia

ISBN: 978-93-6208-050-9 (PB)
First Published, 1894

2nd Impression 2024

Printed at: Gyan Press, Delhi.

AN UNRECORDED CHAPTER OF THE INDIAN MUTINY
Author: REGINALD G. WILBERFORCE

AN UNRECORDED CHAPTER OF THE INDIAN MUTINY.

THE CASHMERE GATE, DELHI.

[*Frontispiece*.

AN UNRECORDED CHAPTER

OF THE

INDIAN MUTINY.

BEING THE PERSONAL REMINISCENCES OF

REGINALD G. WILBERFORCE,

LATE 52ND LIGHT INFANTRY.

COMPILED FROM A DIARY AND LETTERS
WRITTEN ON THE SPOT.

WITH ILLUSTRATIONS.

LONDON:
JOHN MURRAY, ALBEMARLE STREET.
1894.

TO THE

Memory

OF

BRIGADIER-GENERAL

JOHN NICHOLSON.

PREFACE.

No introduction to this little account of what I saw of the great Sepoy Mutiny of 1857 can be more appropriate than a short account of the glorious regiment with which I was permitted to serve. The 52nd Light Infantry was the first regiment in the English army that was distinguished from other regiments by the affix of "Light Infantry."[1] The discipline of the regiment was admi-

[1] Sir John Moore, who in 1801 became Colonel of the regiment, writes in 1805, on his being made K.C.B., "As a Knight of the Bath I am entitled to supporters. I have chosen a Light Infantry soldier for one—being Colonel of the First Light Infantry Regiment."

rable, though it was undoubtedly severe. Inaugurated as it was by that distinguished soldier, General Sir John Moore, of whom it is said "that his life was spent among the troops," it had been continued and perfected throughout the long struggle in the Peninsula, in which campaign the 52nd bore such a distinguished part, and from thence this discipline was brought down to the day I joined the regiment. Part of this discipline was the annual training; officers below the rank of captain, and privates, had to go through the entire drill system, beginning with the goose-step, once a year. It was never considered that a man *knew* his drill, no matter how long he might have been in the regiment. The captains had to go through a certain amount of this annual training, but they were supposed to know the very elementary parts, except indeed they had come from another regiment.[1] Another rule was that no subaltern under a year's standing at head-quarters was allowed to speak or laugh loudly at mess.[2]

The exclusiveness of the regiment was shown by a rule that no one could be made an honorary member of the mess, he might be a mess guest, but not an honorary member; the only exception to this rule was that all officers past or present of the 43rd Light Infantry and the Rifle Brigade were honorary members of our mess, as we were of theirs. There was a feeling in the regiment common to both officers and men, not that they were

[1] A captain who had exchanged to us from the "Guards," and who had been all through the Crimean War, joined the regiment at Lucknow—he was sent to "goose-step."

[2] At the mess table the same formalities in addressing a senior that characterised the parade ground had to be observed.

intrinsically better than other regiments, but that they were guardians of an heritage of fame such as no other regiment possessed,[1] the glories earned on many a hard-fought field culminating in their share of the great victory of Waterloo.[2] So highly did we all esteem the honour of the regiment that we cheerfully submitted to the severe discipline, so that if the time of trial should come, we might be found worthy successors of those men who had left their laurels in our keeping. How well the character of the regiment had been maintained through all the years of peace that had elapsed since it was last in action[3] can be

[1] The "Historical Record of the 52nd Light Infantry," by Captain Moorsom (Bentley, 1860), gives a full account of the doings of the regiment.

[2] The charge on the Young Guard of France is the subject of a picture which adorns the head of the staircase of the Junior United Service Club.

[3] At Waterloo.

gathered from what the Commander-in-Chief in India, the Honourable George Anson, said in 1856. After inspecting the regiment he writes: "*November* 21, 1856.—This battalion under Colonel Campbell manifests all those superior qualifications for which it has been highly distinguished, in peace and war, throughout the present century."

In common with others, I was intensely proud of my regiment. I can never forget the words of the late Duke of Richmond, himself an old officer of the 52nd. In 1856, shortly after I had been transferred to the 52nd by Lord Hardinge,[1] then Commander-in-Chief, I was at Gordon Castle. While there the

[1] Lord Hardinge wrote to my father, "If you do not object to your son going out to India, I have an opportunity of transferring him from the 9th Regiment to the 52nd Light Infantry, quite the best regiment in the service."

old Duke said to me, "Always remember, in everything you do, that you are an officer of the most illustrious regiment in the English army," and I still recall the pride that I felt when I, an ensign who had not passed his drill, was given just before we left Delhi, on account of the lack of officers, the temporary command of one of the companies of the regiment.

There were no special correspondents with the Moveable Column of the Punjaub, and though I do not pretend to give a full account of all John Nicholson's marvellous performances, yet any episode in the life of this great man, to whose memory justice has never been fully done, cannot fail to be of interest. It will be remembered that he was one of the men selected by Lord Dalhousie to settle the Punjaub.

This little book does not aim at giving a full history even of the Moveable Column, far less of the great Mutiny itself. The events recorded in it are taken from a diary, supplemented by a number of letters written at the time to my father, which letters he carefully preserved. All I have attempted to do is to give an account of those stirring days, and of some of the scenes in which I was an actor—not as history, but as they presented themselves to the mind of a boy of only nineteen years old.

CONTENTS.

CHAPTER I.

CHAPTER II.

CHAPTER III.

CHAPTER VII.

CHAPTER VIII.

LIST OF ILLUSTRATIONS.

CHAPTER I.

> "The sudden trumpet sounded as in a dream
> To ears but half awaked, then one long roll
> Of autumn thunder and the jousts began."
>
> THE LAST TOURNAMENT.

January 23, 1857.—In the early morning the good ship *Bengal*, of the Peninsular and Oriental Company, dropped her anchor outside Fort William at Calcutta. Her passengers, of whom I was one, soon landed, and on my nineteenth birthday I found myself in the capital of the land of the pagoda tree. I had come out to India to join my regiment, the 52nd Light Infantry, who when I landed were on the march from Lucknow to Sealkote in the Punjaub. At the Great

Eastern Hotel where I put up, I found a brother ensign, and we agreed to go up country together. Travelling in India was not as simple in those days as it now is, and route arrangements—laying the dâk, as it was termed—had, even on the Grand Trunk Road, to be made some days beforehand. The railway only went some 120 miles from Calcutta, and from the railway terminus carriages were necessary.

During the few days I stayed in Calcutta I dined at Government House with Lord Canning, the then Governor-General of India, to whom I had letters of introduction. At that dinner I met Stewart, who was head of the Telegraph Department, and whose marvellous escape from a tiger is so well described in "The Old Shekarry." I heard him telling Lord Canning of the mysterious night fires, of disaffected men, of sinister language, of veiled warnings; at the time these words made little impression upon me, but when, a few months later, the Mutiny broke out, then the conversation I had listened to came back with full force, and I saw the solution of what then appeared mysterious.

In Calcutta I was a witness of a remarkable scene. One day we heard a great noise and shouting, and saw the street filled with a motley crowd of men of many nations. The reason of the disturbance was soon disclosed: they were pursuing a man, a sailor, who had been detected, almost red-handed, in the murder of a woman in one of the low parts of the town; the enraged crowd were about to lynch the man, whom they had overtaken just outside our windows, when suddenly the culprit made a masonic sign; it was immediately recognized, a large number of men in the crowd began shouldering their way to the man, got to him, surrounded him, kept off others, and finally, having got him away in safety, handed him over to the police to be tried and punished in the regular way.

On January 27th we left Calcutta and its mosquitoes behind us and started for our journey up the country to Umballa, where we expected to find the regiment. Nothing sensational happened to us. We went through the usual experiences of those days: we had the horses who would not start save for a straw fire under them, and who then dashed off for their ten-mile stage at top speed; we met at the dâk bungalows, or staging houses, the same urbane, smiling khitmagar, who in answer to the usual question of "What can we have to eat?" rapidly ran through every conceivable comestible, ending of course with the inevitable fowl, whose chase, capture and slaughter we regularly witnessed. We stayed a day or two at Benares to see the temples and the monkeys, but, with this exception, we made our way up country as quickly as we could, passing Allahabad, Cawnpore, where such ghastly scenes were soon to be enacted, and the strong fortified city of Delhi, the fortifications of which, designed by skilful English engineers, were as strong as science could make them.

Close to Umballa we came upon a detachment of our men with three subalterns, marching up country to join the regiment. We stayed a night with them, and the next day Wingfield and I reported ourselves at head-quarters at

Umballa. We found the regiment in the midst of the excitement of a cricket match against the Station; the first day had gone badly for the regiment, but the Colonel declared that he was not going to march if we were defeated, but would stay on and play a return match. For this there was no necessity; in the second innings the regiment was invincible, and a grand score was made. On February 14 I joined the famous Fifty-second, of whose deeds I had heard so much, and to have been a member of which is a distinction that I cherish to this day.

In these *fin de siècle* days, when the old "numbers" are things of the past, it is something to be able to look back with pride to the fact that I was a member of a regiment of which Sir W. Napier, the historian of the Peninsular War, writes as "a regiment never surpassed in arms, since arms were first borne by men." A regiment not distinguished by a long territorial title, but known on the deathless scroll of fame as "the 52nd."

On February 19 the regiment left Umballa *en route* for Sealkote. I took my first turn with the Colours, which, during the year 1857, my brother ensigns and I carried 1,268 miles. Of carrying those colours I had a good deal more than my fair share; there were only four ensigns altogether with the regiment, but I never missed my turn from sickness or any other cause. In those days a custom prevailed in the army, and for aught I know continues still, called "wetting the colours;" in plain English this means, standing champagne to the mess on first carrying the colours. As we were on the march this was postponed until our arrival at our destination.

In another regiment, one of these "Colour" nights nearly ended in a Court-martial; the giver of the wine was orderly officer of the day, and as such had to visit the guards at night. He left the mess apparently quite sober, but the fresh air outside, acting on the wine he had drunk, caused him to fall off his pony, and he slept in the ditch by the road-side. Some half hour after his Colonel, a very big man, came by on his way to bed; he saw the prostrate ensign, and after trying to awaken him, put him on his shoulders and carried him round the various guards, finally putting him to bed. Next day the report had to be written, and the report stated that the guards had not been visited at night. About noon the Adjutant appeared and requested his immediate attendance at the orderly room. There the Colonel sat looking very stern. "Mr. ——, I see your report omits to mention that you visited the guards last night. What is the reason?" —— hung his head; he was not going to lie, and say that he was taken ill. The Colonel again spoke: "I do not understand this, for I see that the sergeants of the Quarter Guard and the Prison Guard state that you turned them out at 12.30 and 12.50 respectively. How do you account for this?" The Colonel, after keeping up the mystery a short time longer, dismissed the orderly room, and walking home with the youngster said, "You may thank your stars that I found you and carried you round last night. Don't do it again."

On May 10th, the first news of the

Mutiny reached us. We had of course heard of disaffection among the Sepoys, but news that mutiny had been successful at the only station in India where the English troops actually outnumbered the Sepoys, appeared to us impossible; but next day the ill tidings were confirmed. The Meerut troops had after looting the station, marched with their drums beating and colours flying to Delhi, had been joined there by the Sepoys in that city, and had got possession of that strongly fortified position.

On May 12th, in spite of the urgent, nay forcible remonstrances of the Brigadier commanding the station of Sealkote, Colonel Campbell, who commanded the 52nd, determined on a bold move. At about 3 A.M. he despatched one company of 100 men, to each of whom had been served out 60 rounds of ammunition, to the artillery lines to seize the guns. The reason of this determination may be found in the fact, that at the military station of Sealkote the disposition of the troops was: at one end a troop of Horse Artillery; next, a Field Battery of Artillery (these latter comprised a certain number of natives); next, a Bengal Cavalry regiment, irreverently styled "Ornamentals" on account of their blue and silver uniform; then two native infantry regiments; and finally ourselves—that is to say, some 3,000 armed natives were between us and the Artillery. As we marched along the lines in the darkness of early morning, we could hear that the Sepoys of the native regiments were lustily singing; no doubt, songs of rejoicing over the deeds of their brothers, who had seized defenceless Delhi, proclaimed the Great Mogul, and inaugurated his reign by brutal murders of English women and children.

We brought the guns back with us. The Horse Artillery were only too delighted to come; they had heard the noise in the Sepoy lines and were expecting an outbreak and a dash for the guns. The Foot Artillery were not so pleased to be brought away, still they had to come, and when once safely inside our lines we turned the guns round, loaded them with grape, and with port fires ready, guarded them till morning was well advanced. The reason of the forcible remonstrances addressed to our Colonel by the Brigadier was,[1] that he said it showed that we distrusted the Sepoys. Looking back on the events of those Mutiny days, nothing

[1] Poor Brigadier Brind paid for his confidence in the loyalty of the Sepoys with his life; when the mutiny broke out at Sealkote, he was shot by a mutineer.

strikes one more forcibly than the confidence that officers who had been long in India reposed in their men, a confidence that, alas! cost many of them their lives. No one could have been more confident of the loyalty of his men than the Colonel of the 9th Bengal Cavalry, and yet after the Mutiny was over we were told, that one very hot night (it was on May 20), when the officers of the 9th Bengal Cavalry entertained a good many guests at their hospitable mess-table — all windows and doors being open to catch any stray breath of air, and every one round the brilliantly-lighted table being distinctly visible to those outside—that in the darkness a number of cavalry troopers with loaded carbines were waiting for an agreed signal from the infantry lines to fire upon us, a signal which fortunately for us never came.

Every post now brought fresh news; the Mutiny was spreading fast; we had a guard of 100 men out every night. On Sunday the 17th we did not go to church, it was not considered safe, so service was held in the schoolroom within our lines, and a guard with fixed bayonets stood just outside the door.

In order to protect us when we were on duty we were furnished with a guard of the 9th Bengal Cavalry to ride round with us at night when we visited the guards. The first guard we visited was the Prison Guard, from which to the Quarter Guard was a long ride over the lonely plain. Just before we left Sealkote I was on duty, and of course had my patrol. On leaving the Prison Guard I noticed that they were drawing very close to me, and in spite of orders continued to approach. Thoroughly alarmed, I turned my pony and led my patrol such a dance, through compounds, over low walls, &c., that I arrived at the Quarter Guard without my attendants, nor did I see them again; they may have meant nothing, but I had not been long enough in India to have a blind belief in the loyalty of the Mussulman, and I infinitely preferred their room to their company.

On the night of May 20, on our return from the dinner which might have had such a tragic ending, we heard that we were to march in a day or two to form the Flying Column. The next two days were busy ones, packing up; the transport allowance for subalterns was limited to one camel each, so all of us subalterns had to double up, as a tent is a camel's full load. All the things we could not take were sent into the Prison, and there placed under a guard of the 46th Native Infantry. Not only were our personal possessions left there, but all the regimental plate, the great gold candlestick, a relic of the Peninsular War, the leaving gifts of generations of officers, in fact everything valuable that the regiment had, except some wonderful Chateau Margaux, was left in the custody of these loyal Sepoys! We did not leave these things willingly; we could not have taken them with us if we had wished. Every officer had to take in his baggage a certain number of spoons and forks, and these, with a few salt-cellars, and two snuff boxes, were all the plate we took with us. The claret, however, we took. What its history was, and how it came into the possession of the regiment no one knew; all sorts of traditions hung round it. It was precious, and the price was in proportion; no one could afford to have it, and there was not much of it. This old claret, I believed at the time, saved me from fever, for after a certain period of marching and counter-marching our already limited transport suffered further reductions; the Colonel, seeing that this precious liquor could not be carried much longer, ordered its prohibitive price to be lowered to the price of ordinary light claret. Then, while it lasted, I used to drink a bottle a day.

CHAPTER II.

> " Wheresoe'er that fiery star
> Blazeth in the van of war,
> Back retire from its ray
> Shield and banner, bow and spear.
> Maddened horses break away
> From the trembling charioteer ;
> The dread of that stern king doth lie
> On all that sleep beneath the sky."
>
> MARRIAGE OF TIRZAH AND AHIRAD.

ON May 25 the regiment left Sealkote to join the Flying Column at Wuzeer-abad ; two companies were left behind, but within a week they rejoined head-quarters. The regiment then was nearly 900 strong, and, with the exception of a few ensigns, there was not a man in it of less than five years' service. Our first experience of hot-weather marching was a dust storm that came on some two hours after we started. We had taken with us from Sealkote the 35th Native

Infantry, and they, with the camels and the bullock carts, were in front. The storm caused a halt; everyone had to lie down, it was impossible to see anything, and the noise of the wind prevented hearing. When daylight came we found ourselves in front; we had actually marched by the 35th Native Infantry, camels, and bullock carts. Dust was over everything, and so penetrating was its nature that even the glass of a hunter watch in my pocket was covered by it.

Just before we got to Lahore, a native infantry regiment, which had been disarmed, broke away, and a young fellow with some 50 Sikhs was sent in pursuit; he caught them up some 125 miles away, and tried to bring them back, but they would not come. He fired upon them, killing a good many, until his men said they would not fire any more, they had so few cartridges left, and were a long way from any troops in a disturbed country. The officer was in a dilemma: he could not let the Sepoys escape, his men were too few in number to march them back to Lahore, setting aside all the difficulties of commissariat, &c. If the Sepoys got to close quarters they were numerous enough to overpower his men. He, however, managed to march them into a building, and when night came on, he stuffed up all the air-holes, so that in the morning, when the doors were opened, there was no one to come out. The Blackhole of Calcutta was repeated in the Punjaub.

On the 27th we got to Wuzeerabad, where we found the rest of the column, and then all together marched to Lahore, where we arrived on June 2. The troops composing the column were:—

The 52nd Light Infantry.
No. 17 Light Field Battery.
16th Irregular Cavalry.
Detachment 2nd Punjaub Cavalry
No. 1 Light Field Battery.
Left wing 9th Bengal Cavalry.
35th Native Infantry.

Brigadier-General Neville Chamberlain was in command of the force.

On June 9 these troops, afterwards known as the "Moveable Column," left Lahore for Umritzur, where we halted for four days. On June 15 we resumed the march, going in a southerly direction. An extract from a letter written on June 16 from Camp Reyah to my father, the Bishop of Oxford, says:—"We don't know where we are to go: some say Delhi, I am sure I hope so; we are all longing for a slap at the niggers, after being marched about in this weather. I believe we are supposed to be waiting for insurgents coming down from Peshawur, and they must cross the river somewhere about this place, and so we shall nail them here. Delhi is the place to which every eye is turned; if the insurgents obtain the least advantage there, the whole of India will rise and join them. It will be very nice for us; we are very weak, and we are taking care of the 35th Native Infantry, and a wing of the 9th Light Cavalry: a very large river[1] in front of us, increasing every day as the snows melt. We are out in a field, and the heat is no joke: 105° at 9 o'clock, 120° at 12, and from 2 to 4 about 130°, which is tremendous; we get under our beds with a wet towel round our heads. You must not expect a letter every mail, for except we halt, it is an impossibility to write, as we march all night and sleep as much of the day as we can. The winds

[1] The Beas river.

are so hot you cannot move out in them, and when they blow at night, which they do when we are marching, it is not particularly pleasant, for they are quite as hot at night as by day. We are hoping to march to-night towards Delhi.

"*Camp Gorana, June* 17.—I believe we go into Jullundur to-morrow, but we know nothing; we cannot stay where we are, as we have no provisions. What a row there will be in England when the news comes, and how the Delhi and Meerut massacres will shock you! Fancy, they boiled a lady, a Captain's wife, alive in *ghee*, melted butter![1] Don't believe what they tell you about their 'caste,' it is not that they are fighting about; it is a long series of grievances, and 'Oude'[2] has topped it. They think the British

[1] One of the stories current at the time.

[2] The annexation of Oude by Lord Dalhousie.

dominion or *Raj* is over, and they have proclaimed the King of Delhi—King of India. If you look in the map, you will see the river Beas: we are 7 miles from it on the Sealkote side, it flows near Jullundur. All the troops are concentrating on Delhi, and if we don't take care, India will have to be retaken. 'Another sortie from Delhi, repulsed—no particulars,' that's the news just come in. I shall write whenever I can. It is getting so hot I must go under my bed now."

It was at the camp before this one that Brigadier-General Chamberlain left us to go to Delhi to take the post of Adjutant-General to the army before Delhi. On June 22 he was succeeded in his command by John Nicholson, the man who was destined to take such a leading part in that most remarkable feat of arms, the capture of Delhi. Unknown outside a small circle, his deeds on the frontier had stamped him as apart from the ordinary run of mankind. He was of a commanding presence, some six feet two inches in height, with a long black beard, dark grey eyes with black pupils (under excitement of any sort these pupils would dilate like a tiger's), a colourless face, over which no smile ever passed, laconic of speech. Sir John Lawrence, the Lieutenant-Governor of the Punjaub, had sent for him from the frontier, and giving him the rank of Brigadier-General,[1] placed him in command of the Moveable Column. Our Colonel who was thus superseded soon recognized the wisdom of the appointment, for no other man could have done what John Nicholson did.

[1] Nicholson's military rank was that of Captain of the 27th Native Infantry.

Nicholson brought with him from the frontier a motley crew called the "Mooltanee Horse;" they came out of personal devotion to Nicholson, they took no pay from the Government, they recognized no head but Nicholson, and him they obeyed with a blind devotion and a faithfulness that won the admiration of all who saw them. These men, some 250 in number, mounted on their wiry ponies, surrounded the column like a web; they rode in couples, each couple within signalling distance of the other, and so circled the column round for many a mile. Nicholson's personal attendant was a huge Pathan, black-whiskered and moustachioed; this man never left his side, he slept across the doorway of Nicholson's tent, so that none could come in save over his body. When Nicholson dined at mess this Pathan stood behind his chair with a cocked revolver in one hand, and allowed none to hand a dish to his master save himself. The story of this man's devotion was, that years before, in one of the many frontier skirmishes, when Nicholson was surrounded by the enemy, this man's father saved Nicholson's life with his own, by throwing himself between Nicholson and a descending sword which must have killed him, and further, in another of these skirmishes, this man was taken prisoner and carried off, when John Nicholson, single-handed, gave chase, and cutting his way through, bore him away in safety across his saddle bow. It may be mentioned here that Nicholson had the reputation of being one of the best swordsmen in India, and his sword had the credit of being the best sword in India. It was presented to him by the Sikh nation.

The story of this gift from the Sikhs

to Nicholson, as it was told us, was that when the Sikhs had decided on presenting Nicholson with the best sword that could be found, they invited their people to send to Peshawur swords to select from; such a vast number were sent, that selection was difficult. At length, by a process of elimination, the number was reduced to three, all of which appeared to be equally excellent. Nicholson was then invited to take his choice of the three, and chose a straight one. Native swords are very seldom straight—they are generally curved. It was generally supposed that this sword was grooved inside and contained quick-silver, so as to increase the force of a direct blow.

It is known that John Nicholson was worshipped by the Sikhs. Their religion admits of repeated incarnations, and this noble, sad-faced man was thought by them to be their god veiled in human flesh. All travellers in India know the Golden Taj at Umritzur, and the Sikhs declared that if Nicholson would openly profess the Sikh religion, they would raise a Taj to him beside which the Umritzur Taj should be as nought. During the time Nicholson was with the column, it was a common sight of an evening to see the Sikhs come into camp in order that they might see him; they used to be admitted into his tent in bodies of about a dozen at a time. Once in the presence, they seated themselves on the ground and fixed their eyes upon the object of their adoration, who all the while went steadfastly on with whatever work he was engaged in, never even lifting his eyes to the faces of his mute worshippers. Sometimes, overcome perhaps by prickings of conscience, or carried away by feelings he could not control, one of them would prostrate himself in prayer. This was an offence, against the committal of which warning had been given, and the penalty never varied: three dozen lashes with the cat-o'-nine tails on the bare back. This they did not mind, but on the contrary, rejoiced in the punishment, for they used to say: "Our god knew that we had been doing wrong, and therefore punished us." A certain tribe on the frontier had openly adopted Nicholson as their deity, and called themselves the Nickelseyn fakirs. When the news was brought to them that Nicholson was dead, the two head men of the tribe committed suicide, but the next in command addressing the remainder, said: "Nickelseyn always said that he was a man like as we are, and that he worshipped a God whom we could not see, but who was always near us. Let us learn to worship Nickelseyn's God." The tribe went into Peshawur, and putting themselves under Christian teachers, were baptized to a man. Truly "their works follow them," for this was probably the only instance in which natives of India *in a body* forsook their old faith, and became Christians on purely disinterested grounds.

Doubtless John Nicholson's face, his reckless bravery, his manner of life, his immunity from death—for it might almost be said that he sought for death, but could not find it—contributed to encourage the superstitions of a superstitious people.

Fully aware of the necessities of the times, a stern sense of duty had made Nicholson expunge the word "mercy" from his vocabulary, yet such was the nature of the man, that one who was in his closest confidence said that often after ordering executions, he would return to his tent and burst into tears. Nicholson was not a letter-writer; on one occasion during the march of the column, Sir John Lawrence, who was anxious for news, sent a peremptory dispatch, at the end of which he said: "You are to inform me without delay—Where you are; what you are doing; and to send a return of courts-martial held upon insurgent natives, with a list of the various punishments inflicted." This drew from Nicholson this answer: he turned over the document he had received, and wrote on it: 1. Name of place where he was; 2, the date; 3, "THE PUNISHMENT OF MUTINY IS DEATH"; and signed it.

A correspondence between Nicholson

and Sir John Lawrence, in which the former strongly urged the Lieutenant-Governor to order H.M. 87th Regiment—then acting as a guard to the women and children collected at the Hill Station of Murree—to join his column and march to Delhi, affords a characteristic illustration of the serious importance Nicholson attached to the situation. In the last paragraph of the letter which closed the correspondence he writes: "When an Empire is at stake, women and children cease to be of any consideration whatever."

Wherever the column halted the telegraph wires were tapped, so that any telegrams that passed up and down the wire were conducted into a small tent, where sat a telegraph clerk with his instrument. This man's weakness was drink, and he had to be guarded by a sentry to prevent his getting liquor over and above his regular allowance. One of the men[1] who acted as sentry over him tells me that he saw Nicholson come one day to the tent and say to the man, "If you let a message pass without taking it off, I will hang you;" and he adds, "And he would have done it, too. I never saw a man like him; he had an eye like a hawk, and I don't know when he ever slept, for he was about night and day."

Nicholson made himself Postmaster-General,[2] and all letters that passed along

[1] Sergeant Knight, at that time a private.

[2] When the Mutiny broke out, Nicholson was at Peshawur, the approach to which from the south is at Attock, on the Indus. At Attock, Nicholson seized the mails, got a number of native letters translated and copied by some Post-office Baboos, and then sent the letters on to their destinations. The copies he made up into separate packets. A Council to consider the situation and what steps should be taken, was assembled at Peshawur. This Council was attended by not only the Commissioner, the Commander of the Forces, and the

the road were intercepted; the native ones read, and sent on to allay suspicion. By these means Nicholson knew all that was in progress, and many a plot did he leave nearly to develop before he took measures to stop it. During the march in the Punjaub there was a wonderful instance of this. It has been said that the 35th Native Infantry marched with the column. On June 25th the column was to arrive at Phillor,[1] a fort on the

leading men, but also by all the Regimental Commanders in the district. One of the questions to be considered by the Council was, what dependence could be placed on the Native Troops. Colonel after Colonel declared that whatever others might be, the soldiers he commanded were loyal to their salt—were devoted to the English—and would shed the last drop of their blood for the Sirkar. When these declarations were over, Nicholson rose, produced his packets of letters, and handed them to each Colonel separately, with, "Perhaps these letters will interest you." It need hardly be added that the packets of letters were treasonable correspondence.

[1] This important fort on the Sutlej river commanded the entrance to the Punjaub. It was on the Grand Trunk Road, and, like most important positions, was garrisoned by Sepoys. Phillor was within the Jullundur command.

Sutlej river; during the march Nicholson came to our Colonel and said, "Can your men out-march these fellows?" meaning the 35th Native Infantry. Campbell said they could; the men quickened step, and in the morning halted on a sandy plain, naked and desert save for a small temple, with its usual clump of trees, which immediately fronted us. The regiment was drawn into line, the troop of Horse Artillery placed in the middle; all were ordered to load, the guns were loaded, and Nicholson rode along the line to give his orders. "In

At Jullundur itself was Colonel Hartley, of H.M. 8th Regiment. Aware of the extreme importance of this post, and fearful lest he should arouse the susceptibilities of the loyal (?) Sepoys, he resorted to stratagem in order to obtain possession of the fort. Under the pretence of laying up a store of horse forage, &c., he sent in several bullock carts laden with grass and straw, in each of which three or four English soldiers were concealed. The carts were admitted into the fort; the soldiers got up; and Phillor was quietly occupied by the English.

a few minutes you will see two[1] Native Infantry regiments come round that little temple. If they bring their muskets to the 'ready,' fire a volley into them without further orders." The same order was given to the Artillery, whose guns were loaded with grape; the men stood at the ready, the gunners with flaming port-fires; the expected regiments came. Nicholson rode to meet them. He spoke to them, there was a moment's hesitation, then their arms were grounded, and all was over. Two thousand men had laid down their arms to seven hundred! Nicholson, between the fires as he was, must inevitably have been killed, either by us or by the mutineers. As self-appointed Postmaster he knew, by the correspondence that passed through

[1] The 33rd Native Infantry from Hoosheyapore joined our line of march at this place.

his hands, that a scheme had been arranged between the two Native Infantry regiments—when miles distant from one another—that when our regiment, who marched unloaded, came to close quarters, they should fire into us, and then that they should march together down to Delhi.

On July 28th the column marched into Jullundur, where Nicholson had arrived the day before, and as it turned off the Trunk Road to march to quarters, one British soldier was overheard to say, "Jack, the General's here."

"How do you know?"

"Why, look there; there's his mark."

The "there" his fellow soldier was told to look at was a pair of gallows, each of which was adorned with six hanging mutineers, while close by were several bullock-carts, all filled with

Sepoys who had revolted, and who were waiting for their turn.

When the column first started under General Neville Chamberlain, courts-martial, drumhead, used to be held, and the mutineers who were found guilty were blown from the muzzles of guns to which they were securely tied. Few courts-martial were held by Nicholson; his dictum, "The punishment of mutiny is death," obviated any necessity for trials; while he himself, with the opportunities he had, or, more properly speaking, the opportunities for judging that he made for himself, coupled with his wonderful power of recognizing a Sepoy, however disguised, relieved the officers of the Moveable Column from an extra duty which was not of the very slightest use.

A remarkable instance of Nicholson's power of penetrating the disguise of a Sepoy happened as the column marched from Goodaspore to attack the mutineers. The low ground, through which the road was carried on an embankment, was partially submerged, it being the rainy season; in marching along the road, two bowed-down wretched-looking men, with bundles on their backs, had, owing to the narrowness of passage, passed close by the regiment. Some half-hour afterwards Nicholson, attended by his Brigade-Major, his Aide-de-camp, and some Pathans, came down the road at a hand-gallop to overtake the column; as he passed the two men he turned slightly round, and, pointing to the two apparently innocent-looking men, said to the Pathans who were following, *Maro!* The order was instantly

[1] Kill.

obeyed; the unerring eye of Nicholson had detected the Sepoy, the harmless-looking bundles they were carrying were native swords, and these were being taken to Goodaspore to arm an irregular cavalry regiment which had been disarmed by Nicholson the previous day.

Nicholson abandoned the practice of blowing mutineers from guns; he thought the powder so expended might be more usefully employed. Once, and once only, did he execute in this fashion—it was just after he joined the column; he had ordered a drumhead court martial for the trial of nine mutinous Sepoys; they were found guilty by the court martial and sentenced to death. A hollow square was formed by the nine guns on one face, the 35th Native Infantry, from whose ranks the mutineers about to suffer had been taken, were drawn up opposite facing the guns : the wings of the regiment made up the remaining sides of the square. The nine guns were unlimbered in open order and loaded with, of course, powder only. When all was ready an order was heard outside the square, "Quick march," and immediately the nine mutineers, with a space between each of them, corresponding exactly to the distance between the guns, marched into the hollow square. At the word "Halt!" each man stopped opposite the muzzle of a gun; "Right face," they turned; "Stand-at-ease," they joined their hands and leant back against the gun. The next instant their heads flew upward into the air, their legs fell forward, and their intestines were blown into the faces of their former comrades who stood watching the scene. Mutineers as they were, no one who saw this execution could refrain from admiring the undaunted courage and coolness with which these men met their death.

On July 4th, as the column was retracing its steps to Umritzur, an incident occurred, owing to an order of Nicholson's, which might have had a disastrous ending. The order was that no natives should be allowed to ride by any white man. They were to be made to get off and salaam. In the very early morning of July 4th, while it was still dark, the orderly officer for the day was, according to custom, riding on in front of the column to pick up the baggage camels, &c., which always started from the last camp some hours earlier, so as to get to the camping ground before the column came in. The orderly officer on duty had to see that the camp was properly ordered. In the darkness he was riding along more than half asleep, roused every now and then by a stumble from his horse, a stumble not unfrequently attended by a fall of both horse and rider, when he was thoroughly awakened by his horse shying violently across the road. He soon discovered that the cause of his horse's agitation proceeded from the approach of an elephant. Pressing his horse close up to the elephant, he called out in English, "Who are you?" Getting no answer, he drew his revolver, and again hailing, said, "Get down, you niggers, and salaam, or I will fire at you!"

It was light enough for him to see that the elephant had a howdah on, and that there was more than one occupant of the howdah. The only reply to the threatening language was a rattle of arms and a rapid whispering, immediately followed by a commanding voice, which ordered something. Down went the elephant on its knees, and from the howdah stepped two figures, who duly salaamed to the young officer. He then rode on, thinking nothing of the incident; but next day Nicholson's brigade-major came to his tent with, "Here, youngster, the General wants to speak to you; what on earth have you been up to?" They both went to Nicholson's tent. The General was sitting, writing at his table; near him stood a native magnificently dressed, with a clear olive complexion, black beard and whiskers. Nicholson said: "You met an elephant on the road this morning, and made the riders get down and salaam to you; why did you do it?"

"Your order, Sir, that no natives should pass a white man riding, without dismounting and salaaming." Nicholson turned to his companion and said something in a language unintelligible to the young officer, and then turning to him, said, "You owe your life to this gentleman, for his attendant would have shot you, but he prevented him." The stranger said something in the same unintelligible language to Nicholson, who then said, "You can go, but before you do so, I may tell you what he has just said to me: 'No wonder you English conquer India when mere boys obey orders as this one did.'" The young officer heard afterwards that the man he had made salaam to him in the darkness of the morning was a trusted emissary of the great Dost Mahommed, the ruler of Cabul, who had sent a great Prince with messages assuring Nicholson of his loyalty to the English in the terrible struggle in which they were engaged, and promising more material aid in the shape of troops should Nicholson ask for them. The fact of the Dost sending the message to Nicholson instead of to Sir John Lawrence, the Lieut.-Governor of the Punjaub, shows how much Nicholson was thought of, even by those who were not under English rule.

Some of the Afghans who were with the column were never weary of declaiming against the cowardice of the Sepoys, who killed women and children. They said: "When we fought against you English we killed men,[1] but we protected your women; *men* do not fight against women, only against men." These men used frequently to come into our mess-tent on invitation, sit down and smoke a cigar, and drink a brandy and soda; one of them was asked, if the doing this

[1] Cf. Lady Sale's Journal.

did not injure his caste. "Caste," he answered, "is only made for dogs like that," pointing to the man who had just served him; "not for chiefs."

On July 6th we got back to Umritzur; we had left it on June 16th. Since then the flame of mutiny had spread: the 59th Native Infantry, who were in charge of the fort, were known to be disaffected. Directly we arrived we marched straight to the gates of the fort, surprised the guard, occupied quietly position after position, marched the 59th Native Infantry out on the plain and disarmed them. So surprised were they that there was not the slightest resistance.

CHAPTER III.

"All was prepared—the fire, the sword, the men
To wield them in their terrible array.
The army, like a lion from his den,
March'd forth with nerve and sinews bent to slay,—
A human Hydra, issuing from its fen
To breathe destruction on its winding way."

DON JUAN.

AT Umritzur we halted until July 10th. That evening, while we were seated round the mess-table, about half-way through dinner, Nicholson, who had not spoken a word, suddenly said, "Gentlemen, I do not want you to hurry your dinner, but the column marches in half-an-hour." This announcement soon set everyone hard at work; dinner was finished in haste, and we were all out of the mess-tent, hurrying to give orders about our things and wondering much what the reason was for this sudden order. We soon heard it—the native troops, which we had left behind us at Sealkote, had broken out into mutiny, released the prisoners from the jail, looted the station, and marched off to Delhi. Nicholson, by a forced march, hoped to intercept them. At 8·30 the column started: eight companies of the regiment, some Punjabees, and Bourchier's troop of Horse Artillery. One of those who shared in that long night march thus describes it: "I could never forget that march. A few of us never went to bed that day, for we did not want to spoil a night's sleep; we had been looking forward to the luxury of that sleep in the darkness; for weeks past we had only slept in the daytime, in the glaring sunshine, shaded it is true by the canvas of our tents; but to sleep in the dark, that was worth keeping awake for; so we kept each other awake in the daytime in anticipation of our sleep. When we started we were pretty tired, and very soon I fell fast asleep on my pony. Suddenly I woke; the pony was standing with his head in a prickly bush. I listened; there was no sound. I called aloud; there was no answer. I had no idea where I had wandered. I was off the road—that was all I knew. I turned the pony's head, the sense of weariness overpowered me, and again I slept. My next awakening was in a different scene: it seemed a wild medley; shouts and squeals filled the air and thoroughly woke me up. I found that I was back on the line of march again and in the middle of the spare artillery horses; why I was not kicked by some of them I know not. I soon found my place with my regiment, and kept fairly awake for the rest of the night."

Early in the morning we halted at a

little village called Buttala; here we ate the food we had brought with us (I only had two thin biscuits, a little brandy, and a bottle of soda-water); then on again in the sun. About 10 we halted again under a gigantic tree, whose great branches, with their pendant uprights, covered so wide an area that under its shade there was room and to spare for the whole regiment. Beside us there was a native, who, with bullocks, was working an irrigation pump of the most primitive pattern: it consisted of an endless rope to which little earthen cups were attached; these, filled with water from the well, were raised by the bullocks and emptied into a trough which ran out into the fields. In about twenty minutes some bread came up for the men; we got a little, so then we had bread and cold water for breakfast. Presently some of the ubiquitous Mooltanee Horse arrived, bringing news, and at midday we started again on the hot and dusty road. While under the tree we had seen our camels pass us; about 5 P.M. we came in sight of our tents, pitched ready for us. I was so tired that I threw myself down on my bed and went to sleep at once, never waking for dinner, and slept on till next morning.

I had ordered breakfast about nine o'clock, and just as I was ready and was leaving my tent for the mess-tent, the fall-in bugle sounded, and I had only time to run back, get my sword and revolver, and fall in, breakfastless. The heat during the previous day had been so excessive that it was difficult to grasp the brass sword-handle; many horses died of sunstroke during that day, many men were invalided, and some died of heat apoplexy on that march of forty-two miles in twenty-one hours, most of it in the full blaze of a July sun. We marched from our camp to have as we knew our first brush with the mutineers, and to see for the first time shots fired in earnest. Just before we came to the place where the action was fought, we had to cross a stream which intersected the road; the officers, who were all riding, were told to dismount and walk through with the men. This we did; the water felt quite warm as we passed through it, many of us seized the opportunity to pour some of the water on our heads, wetting them thoroughly. On the other side we halted and formed line, and the guns were unlimbered.

To our front there was a line of trees, fringing the Ravee river, and under those trees the mutineers were drawn up in line waiting for us, the 46th Native Infantry, about 1,000 strong, and a wing of the 9th

Bengal Cavalry, which was stationed on their left. Our force consisted of about 220 of all ranks. So serious had the effects of the heat been on that day and the one before upon the men, that during the twelve-mile march our men fell out of the ranks by scores, and were carried after us in dhoolies; of course the nine guns of Bourchier's troop were with us, and some so-called Sikhs, in reality Punjabees. Nicholson now rode up; he at once ordered the guns to limber up again and get to closer quarters. This was done, and the next time we halted we were only about 100 yards from the mutineers, who took the initiative and fired a volley into us and then charged with their cavalry on our right flank, while their infantry attacked our left flank.

These Sealkote mutineers had seen

us march out of the station dressed in white, but while we were at Lahore our Colonel ordered all the clothes to be dyed with a colour which afterwards became so well known in India as *Kharkee;* it was a capital colour, and almost invisible. During a long march it would have been impossible to keep the white clothes clean: it looked neat and certainly deluded the mutineers. They had broken out into mutiny on July 9th, and, allowing for the necessary time to elapse, they calculated that no white troops could have got to where we were; besides, they knew that the so-called Sikh police were dressed in *Kharkee*, and, as far as they knew, the English troops were clad in white.

On the right the cavalry were received in squares of companies; they rode round and round, firing their pistols point blank at us; at length they had had enough and retired. In doing so, one cavalry trooper seized an artilleryman by his shoulder-belt and was riding away with him, when they crossed the path of fire of one of the nine-pounders; at that instant the charge of grape was fired, it struck the three of them at a distance of some fifteen yards, blowing the horse, the rider and the captive literally to pieces.

It ought to have been stated that the formation of our attack was the nine guns at wide intervals, the regiment being divided up between them.

While the cavalry were thus busy on our right, one or two episodes occurred. Nicholson, and some of his Pathan body-guard, were behind us. It is the creed of these men that to be in action without individually accounting for some one is a matter of shame. In pursuance of this doctrine, we saw two of the body-guard come out on our right and apparently challenge two of the Bengal Cavalry to single combat; anyway, the challenge was accepted, and the four rode at each other, the Pathans on their ponies, their tulwars waving in circles round their heads, their loose garments flowing; the Bengalees sat erect on their big horses, their swords held ready to deliver the "point," a stroke no irregular cavalry man comprehends, as he does not in his sword exercise learn to parry the thrust. For a moment all eyes were on the four combatants: the thrust was delivered, but instead of piercing the bodies of the Pathans it passed over them, for they threw themselves back on their ponies, their heads on the crupper, their feet by the ponies' ears, and in that position swept off the heads of the Bengal Cavalry men; instantly the ponies wheeled round, the men straightened themselves in their saddles, and they passed away from our vision. Then Nicholson came into view; he too was going to kill his man. The scene was a brief one, the mutineer thrust at the great swordsman, who parried the thrust, and with apparently the same motion clove his assailant's head in two; he also passed away from our sight.

In the smoke and noise it was impossible to see what was going on on our left, but soon an urgent message reached us, our square opened out, and with fixed bayonets we charged down on the left. We found that owing to the before-mentioned delusion on the part of the Sepoys, their charge on our left had been so spirited that our men had been driven in on the centre. The tide was soon turned, but this was probably the only instance in the Mutiny when Englishmen and Sepoys actually crossed bayonets in the open. I saw one Sepoy pierced through with a bayonet, and borne to the ground, the bayonet going into the ground and twisting so that it could not be withdrawn. One of our men, an Irishman, who was also a spectator of this incident, immediately took off his bayonet, and, putting it in the ground, went on with his butt, which he flourished to some purpose, one swing of it felling no less than three of his opponents. The Sepoys were forced backward, and breaking, fled to the river in confusion, leaving, however, many dead and wounded in their flight.

While we were thus engaged another action was going on in our rear. The cavalry which had been driven off, rode down the very road we had come along, and in so doing they encountered our sick, who were slowly following. As soon as the bearers of the dhoolies saw the Sepoy Cavalry coming they promptly put the dhoolies down and bolted. A sergeant took command: quickly getting the dhoolies across the road he formed the men behind them, and from this comparatively safe position fired into the advancing cavalry, with such effect that again the cavalry had to turn and seek safety in some other direction. Our total loss was 2 officers and 25 men killed and wounded; of the wounded, one was the Colonel, and the other a subaltern, who was hit in the chest with a spent bullet; he saw the hole in his jacket and immediately concluded that he was shot through the lungs, so he began to make his way to the rear. In doing this he encountered the Brigade-Major, who hailed him, asking what the matter was. "I am shot through the lungs," was the answer. The Brigade-Major, who knew that a person shot through the lungs could hardly speak with so sound a voice, said: "Turn round and let me see the hole where the bullet came out." This was done, and the desired position being also attained, the Brigade-Major with a lusty smack on the back ordered him back again to the front.

On that day I shall never forget the thirst that I suffered, and great was my joy when I espied a well. I longed to get a draught of water, but our doctor would not let me drink; he, however, dropped some of the water on my tongue, which was much swollen. The water felt so cold that it almost hurt. The next year a brother officer and I were going to the hills on sick leave. On our journey we had to pass this very well. I told him of the marvellous cold of the water in that well, and we both, thirsty though we were, abstained from drinking anything in anticipation of the glorious cold draught we should get from this wonderful well. When, however, we got to the well, we found the water of the usual tepid temperature, and I then knew that it was only the extremity of thirst which had made me, the year before, think it ice-cold. Just before we marched back to the camp we had left in the morning, I saw a sergeant come up to one of the officers to make his report of the casualties in his company. He presented the paper, and no sooner had he done so than he spun round on his heels and fell dead from sunstroke.

Right glad we all were to be back again in camp, and I was especially glad to be once more at the mess table, and to eat the first food that had crossed my lips for forty-eight hours, during which time we had marched sixty-six miles, fought our first action, and been exposed for two successive days to the blazing heat of an Indian July sun. We halted in camp two days, during which numbers of prisoners of all sorts were brought in, both by the Sikh Police and the Mooltanee Horse; they used to be paraded in a line in the evening, and then Nicholson would walk down the line. Every now and then he pointed to a man, who was immediately taken out. Those pointed at were Sepoys, and ordered for instant execution; the remainder, mere country people, were let go.

On July 15th we marched again down the same road to our former battle-field. We got there in the evening. Clouds of vultures rose from or hopped about on the ground; they had been satiating themselves with the dead Sepoys and with dead horses; the stench as we marched across the scene of the encounter was horrible. Our tents were soon pitched inside the belt of trees where we first saw the mutineers. Many of us took the opportunity to go down to the banks of the river, where the nine-pounders were firing at an island to which the Sepoys had retreated, and where they had the old twelve-o'clock gun from the station. While we were there watching what was going on we saw the Sepoys drive some camels into the river. The stream shoaled considerably on the island side, while on our side the water was very deep; we noticed that the camels were loaded with small boxes. When well out in the stream we saw the cords that held the boxes cut, and the boxes fall into the water. We afterwards found out that it was our regimental plate we saw drowning; we had left it behind, for means of transport were scanty. The boxes sank in the shifting sands of the river, and although for two winters, when the rivers are low, we had numbers of men with long iron probes searching, no part of the plate was ever again found, and the regiment suffered an irreparable loss.

That evening one of our poor fellows shot himself; he was cleaning one of the officers' revolvers, and in showing the mechanism to a brother soldier the pistol went off and killed him instantly. As I was on duty that day I had to bury him. He was sewn up in his bedding, a grave was dug, the firing party told off, and I took the funeral, the first but not the last on service. It was a solemn scene—the wide desolate plain deserted by everything except the gorging vultures and the howling jackals. I read part of our beautiful burial service, beginning at "Man that is born of a woman;" then three volleys were fired, and all was over; we marked the place by a wooden cross, but next year when I passed by even this little record was gone.

The next morning we paraded at 3 A.M.; of course it was pitch dark. As soon as we had fallen in, the Colonel arrived, mounted on a small pony he had borrowed, as he did not want to take his charger over the river in the boat. He called the regiment to "attention," and gave the order "Shoulder arms." In those days the custom was to throw the musket up and bring the right hand down on the butt with a smack; the order was promptly obeyed, and as every hand came down simultaneously, the pony, unused to martial exercises, turned suddenly round, depositing the Colonel on the ground. After the Colonel had recovered from his somewhat undignified position, we marched down to the banks of the river; there we found two large flat-bottomed boats, and in them we crossed over in detachments. Meanwhile our field-guns were firing away across the river at the Sepoy position.

Our company was the leading company of the day; during the march we always took the leading position in turn, for as a rule the dust on the line of march was very bad. We were extended in skirmishing order and told to advance. Of course we had supports behind us. The Captain was on the right, and I was on the left; the ground was level and at first covered with high rushes, but these soon gave way to grass, and then we saw the object of attack—an earthwork—in which was our old twelve-o'clock gun. The mutineers kept firing at us as we advanced, but we could hear the shots singing far above our heads. While we thus advanced Nicholson joined us; he rode by me, and as he rode told me a story of how he had killed a tiger on horseback with his sword—I think he said on that very island, but I may be mistaken. The feat was performed by riding round and round the tiger at a gallop, gradually narrowing the circle until at last the swordsman was near enough to deliver his blow. Of course he had only the one blow. It is well known that Sir James Outram, the Bayard of India, performed this feat. During the circling process the tiger does not spring upon the horseman, probably because he is watching his opportunity, and as the circle draws in upon him he gets more and more bewildered by the, to him, strange manœuvre. Every sportsman knows that when a covey of partridges settles in the middle of a field of turnips, no matter how wild they are, they can always be approached by walking round and round them, gradually narrowing the circle, and when flushed they will get up singly or in pairs, screaming and twisting in their attempts to escape.

When about 200 yards distant from the gun they fired grape at us; we closed on our centre, leaving a gap for the fire of the gun, charged, and in a few moments took the gun. A revolver given me by my father saved my life, for being a fast runner, and from my position in front having a start, I was over the bank on the left just before my Captain jumped in on the right, and was brought up by a huge horse-pistol held to my forehead. I fired instantly, not aiming, and the bullet went through my assailant's heart, the discharge of his pistol blowing off my solar topee. All the Sepoys but one in charge of that gun died at their post; the one who ran away was pursued by Nicholson, who overtook him, and rising in his stirrups dealt him such a mighty blow that he actually severed the man in two! It is curious to relate that Nicholson, who hated Sepoys[1] with a hatred that

[1] By "Sepoy" is meant the old Company's Sepoy. Nicholson loved his Mooltanees, Pathans, and Afreedis.

no words could describe, not only had them buried according to the rites of the Mussulman religion, but actually raised a monument on the spot where the defenders of the gun fell, and placed an inscription on it, testifying his regard for their valour. The clearing of the island was speedily accomplished; most of the Sepoys sought for safety in the swollen waters of the Ravee and found death, only a very few being captured and of course shot.

One or two incidents however occurred: the first was when one of our supports reached us they perceived a figure standing on the edge of the river; excitement multiplied the solitary figure into many, and the company deploying into line fired a volley. When the smoke cleared away the figure was still there, untouched, uninjured, and a closer examination revealed the fact that there were two persons—one a woman, and the other a baby in arms. The other incident happened in this wise: a lot of us youngsters saw a small house, one of the few dwelling-places situated on the island, and to it we repaired to see what was inside. There was nothing visible, the one room of the little house was empty; the room had a plank ceiling, and while we were standing about talking some one heard or thought he heard a noise above the planks. Placing therefore his revolver in a crack of the planks he fired, and on search discovered he had killed a Sepoy who had selected that place for his refuge, and would doubtless have escaped had not nature compelled him to reveal himself.

Almost directly after this we were ordered to march down to Delhi, and we were all much rejoiced, for the weariness of the constant marching backwards and forwards in the Punjaub was very trying, and we were longing to be present at the place where the great drama was to be played out. Everyone knew that whether India was to be held or whether it would have to be reconquered depended on the taking of Delhi. If we failed, the whole country would have risen in arms against us, whereas at present only the Sepoys had risen.

CHAPTER IV.

> "Hearken to the steady stamp!
> Mars is in their every tramp;
> Not a step is out of tune."
>
> THE DEFORMED TRANSFORMED.

ON July 27, a letter written from Camp, Kurtalpore, says: "We are longing to hear how you take this Mutiny in England. I suppose people will say, Oh, Delhi can't stand a week. How sold they will be! they have been besieging Delhi two months now and cannot take it. We march to Jullundur to-night. We are just in camp and have got our tents pitched, and had something to eat. The wind is blowing deliciously—if it only would not blow my paper about, and it is so very hard to write on one's bed. I hope it won't rain very hard to-day, as my tent is on low ground, and two hours will make it a swamp. As we were marching this morning, it was pitch dark, and I could not see where I was going. I suddenly found myself head over ears in water—a pleasant thing, certainly, when I had to march on in these wet things. Our army before Delhi is in a dreadful state—nothing to drink. The water cannot be drunk there. Beer is 28 rupees (£2 16*s.*) a dozen, and soda-water about six shillings a dozen. We are buying up everything for the mess as we go down, both eatables and drinkables.

"We have just been reading a letter in the *Times* about 'the mild and ductile Hindoo!' The atrocities they have committed beat everything that has ever been heard of; the other day the niggers took a man prisoner, and drew all his nails out, and then boiled him alive in oil! I most sincerely trust that the order given when we attack Delhi will be what was given to us on the 12th—'Kill every one; no quarter is to be given.' I hear they offered to treat with the King of Delhi for terms, and his answer was: 'Free passage for all Europeans to Calcutta.'[1]

"One of our men named Kingsley, who is the tallest man in the regiment, volunteered last night to carry the fire-lock and ammunition of a comrade who was not well. His rear-rank man heard the men approve this action, and say what a good thing it was to be so tall and so strong, and sung out: 'Here, one of you fellows hand me your musket and ammunition.' When he had got them, he marched along with his double load, and said: 'These long fellows

[1] It will be remembered that the Nana made a similar offer to General Wheeler before the Cawnpore Massacre.

shan't have it all their own way; I'll show you that a little 'un is as good as they!' The small man is my soldier servant, called Howorth, and comes from Lancashire."

From the day we started from our station at Sealkote in May until our arrival in the camp before Delhi on August 14, we had marched altogether 900 miles, and only in the latter part of the journey were there any conveyances; then we had bullock carts for just half the regiment, so half were carried, and the other half walked. Officers and men were served alike; for instance, there was one bullock cart allotted to eight subalterns, the cart held four. The first night we had this cart we put the colours into it, as the carrying them was very wearisome, for, besides being heavy, they were so unwieldy. All went well that night, but the next evening, when we were putting them in the cart, the Colonel appeared, with "What, put the colours of my regiment in a bullock cart!" We were ordered instantly to take them out, and for the rest of the journey they were duly carried.

The most irksome duty we had was treasure guard; the troops before Delhi had no money, and so we brought them down a considerable amount. This treasure, all in rupees, was carried on camels, and a guard of 100 men with a Captain and subaltern had to march with the camels. Now, a camel is a useful beast of burden, but he is a beast in more senses than one to march with, for his pace is two miles an hour, the most wearisome pace in the world. No one who has ever marched for twenty miles with camels—keeping pace, that is to say, with them—is ever likely to forget his experience. The treasure guard always started first and always got into camp last. Then, all day long, sentries had to be visited, guards inspected, until the happy time arrived when the relief came, and the boxes of rupees were handed over to some one else's custody.

Our regular marches, before the forced ones, were very different. As a general rule we marched between 12 and 1 A.M., our band playing us out of camp on to the Trunk Road with "The girl I left behind me;" then the order was given to "March at ease," "March easy." The men used to sling their firelocks over their shoulders and smoke their pipes. The band used to go on playing, and when the bandsmen were tired, our bugle band would take it up and play away. When they had finished, some individual, somewhere in the centre of the regiment, would start a song, and so the hours whiled away till "coffee shop." Half way along the line of march we always halted for half an hour; the men had rum served out to them, and the officers used to have coffee as well as other things. One of the favourite songs was of a most revolutionary character; it had about 30 verses and a long chorus. I forget the song, but I recollect that "Confound our officers!" held a place in the chorus, and used to be lustily shouted. At first the men would not sing this song—they thought it would hurt our feelings, but it had so good a tune that nearly every night one of our Captains would call for it. One capital song began—

"For our broadswords shall glitter, and our grape-shot shall fly,
Before the French shall come and drink old England dry.
(*Chorus*) Drink old England dry."

Another was—

> "As we were marching down the street
> We heard the people say,
> There goes a gallant regiment;
> They are now marching away.
>
> Away go those brave heroes,
> The like we never see more,
> And with them goes the light bobbee,
> The lad that I adore."

And one more—

> "Neither pot nor pipe shall grieve me,
> Nor yet disturb my mind,
> When I come rolling home
> To the girl I left behind.
>
> (*Chorus*) Happy is the girl that will keep me
> When I come rolling home."

Coffee-shop over, there was more music, and so the march went merrily on through the night hours, for soon after we saw the great round red sun loom upwards from the horizon we reached the camp, which was always nearly ready. The first thing to be done was a good wash, to get rid of the dust of the march, and then every one turned in to sleep. At first we used to sleep on our beds, but we soon gave this up, the heat was too great, 130° Fahr. We used to sleep under our beds to keep the heat of the sun off.

One day, while we were all asleep, a tremendous rain-storm burst over us. We were awakened by getting wet, and soon the camp was alive with everyone in all kinds of costume, searching for and occasionally pursuing down some rivulet their shoes, stockings, and other garments which had been left on the ground in the tent. About 12.30 we began to get up, and 1 to 1.30 found us all gathered together in the big mess tent, the temperature of which, by the aid of *tatties*, we managed to keep down to 120°, for breakfast.

Amongst us youngsters, after breakfast, the question was "What shall we do?" Some one, who was supposed to know—

who it was I know not—had said that the sun in India never hurt anyone during his first year: the amount of cool blood in our veins was enough to counteract any extra heating power. Anyway, whether this dictum was true or not, nearly every fine day, and we had plenty of them, some of us, and I always amongst the number, used to get on our ponies about 3 P.M. and scour the surrounding country in search of antelope, nylghau, or even the familiar pariah dog; the two former we tried to shoot; I think we once got a blue bull; the latter—and they never failed us—we used to try and stick with spears. On one occasion we had a duty ride; it was during the forced march, bullocks for the carts were wanted, and volunteers were asked for to procure some. Another youngster and I started off to a village some miles from the line of march; we could neither of us speak Hindustani, our knowledge of the language being confined to a very few words. However, we wrote down what we were to ask for, and after a little practice got the pronunciation right. Thus armed we arrived at the village, a very fair sized one; we at once asked for the head man, and on his appearance read him our demand. He made us understand that he had no bullocks, and could not get any. We knew that this was untrue, and again and again repeated our demand. By this time a considerable crowd had collected round us, and we noticed that they all carried long bamboos shod with iron. They were closing in upon us and the headman, and the situation was getting dangerous. "How are we ever going to get out of this?" asked my companion. I told him we had better ride at them as hard as we could, and so try and get through. Accident, however, came to our aid and saved us; for to ride through the circle would have been impossible; we were both unarmed, save for our riding crops. As I turned to speak to my companion, I put my hand on my horse's back just behind the saddle, the horse resented this with a kick; here then was our opportunity, and I was not slow to avail myself of it. Iron-shod heels *v.* iron-shod bamboos! The heels won easily, the circle widened and widened until at last I could suspend the provocation to kick, and we rode away without our bullocks but with whole skins.

As a sequel to the story, when we returned to camp, and told our story, a few Pathans succeeded where we had failed; their persuasions, however, were of such a pressing nature, that that particular headman ruled no more over the destinies of that village.

At 6 P.M. there used to be a short parade, and at 7.30 we were all gathered together round the mess table for dinner. While that meal was in progress, camp was struck and the camels loaded to be sent forward in readiness for the next day. The mess tent was the last to be taken down. After dinner we lay down on the ground, wet or dry, to smoke our pipes and get some two hours' sleep before resuming the march.

One night we were all waiting for our dinner and none appeared, messengers were sent to the cooking tent, but only brought back word that dinner was coming, till about half an hour after the appointed time, Nicholson, who always dined with us, came on the scene, with

"I am sorry, Gentlemen, to have kept you waiting for your dinner, but I have been hanging your cooks!"

We soon learnt the story. One of the cook boys, whose conscience revolted at wholesale murder, went to Nicholson and told him that the soup was poisoned with aconite. Nicholson kept the boy safe until just before dinner was to be served, when he sent for and arrested the cooks. The soup was brought in with the cooks. Nicholson told one of the cooks to eat some; the cook protested, on the ground of caste. Nicholson knew that a Mussulman had no caste, and peremptorily ordered the cook to swallow some, telling him at the same time that he, Nicholson, knew it was poisoned; of course the cook denied this. Nicholson then had a small monkey brought in, and some of the soup poured down its throat. In a few minutes the truth of the cook boy's story was seen—the little monkey was dying of poison. Sentence of death was at once passed, and a few minutes afterward our regimental cooks were ornamenting a neighbouring tree.

At a camping ground, either the next or the one after this incident—anyway, it was on August 10—we halted for a night after a very long and trying march. The place we were at was a noted place for thieves, and we were all duly warned to be extra careful that night. Among the regimental possessions were two bull-dogs, the property of one of the officers, and we surmised that the thieves, if they had any intention of paying us a nocturnal visit, would certainly take the precaution of ascertaining if there were any dogs about, and if so, where they were located, and would avoid that particular tent. The result proved the correctness of our surmise. When night came, the dogs were separated, and placed in two tents different from the one they had occupied during the day. About 1 A.M. a tremendous noise was heard, and "Billy," the plate-faced bull-dog, was found with his teeth fixed in the throat of a thief in one of the tents. The man, naked as he was born, and oiled all over, had crept through the line of sentries into camp, through the native servants, who lay round the tents and inside the tent, to steal what he could find; he was unarmed, save for a long knife he carried in his hand, with which he had wounded "Billy," though not seriously.

Years after I happened, while shooting, to come across one of these thief villages. The inhabitants were all thieves, and were all trained to their work as children by the "Fagin" of the place. I had a good many deer on the elephants when I arrived at the village, and not wanting so much fresh meat for the camp, I distributed what there was to spare among the people who had come up to see the camp and the stranger Englishman who had come to invade their jungle solitude. That night, my bearer told me that we had indeed "fallen among thieves," so I ordered men to walk round and round my tent in order to guard it, the men to be relieved every two hours. In the morning I was pleased to find that nothing was missing. Next evening, as I was sitting by my fire after the day's shooting, the head man of the village came up and entered into conversation with me. After a bit it took this turn.

"Why did the Sahib guard his tent last night?"

"Because I heard that there were many thieves in the village."

"Did the Sahib think that those guards would protect him?"

I told him that of course I did. The man smiled and told me that the meat I had given them protected me; that having partaken of my hospitality they would not rob me. I was then incredulous and told the man as much, upon which he said that he would, if I liked, give an object lesson, and that they would take anything I chose to name out of my tent that night—of course restoring it next morning. I accepted the challenge, and named my watch under my pillow, saying that I would not hold myself responsible for any damage that might happen to the thief, and that if I found him out I would certainly shoot him. The head man assented, saying that if the thief bungled, it would serve him right to be shot. He then told me a good deal of their ways, of how they passed stolen property on from one hand to another by means of runners through the jungle, till they got it safely into the receiver's hands. "But are not," I asked, "your runners ever killed by tigers in the jungle at night?" He said such a thing had never happened, and accounted for this immunity by the fact that the smell of the oiled preparation with which their bodies were anointed so jarred upon the tiger's olfactory nerves that he left them alone. That night my guards were all duly warned that an attempt would certainly be made, and a promise of liberal *backsheesh* was made for detection or prevention. Of course in the morning my watch was missing, and of course it was duly restored to me by a young thief who was brought into my presence by the head man, and who, if his dark skin had permitted, would doubtless have blushed when I complimented him on his adroitness and rewarded him duly for his dexterity.

On July 26th we had again to cross the Beas river. The engineers reported the bridge of boats fairly safe; it might last long enough for us to go over, it might go at any moment. We were ordered to cross over by companies, and in single file; this naturally occupied a considerable time. As we went over we could see and feel the boats rising and falling, hear them creaking and grinding together as the swollen river lifted them up or swayed them to and fro; we all got safely over, and halted on the opposite bank. The elephants came next; they tried the bridge before venturing on it, and declined to trust themselves on the frail structure, preferring to go through the river rather than over the bridge. Then came the long procession of camels; they got over all right, but even our unscientific eyes could see that the boats could not hold together much longer.

Just then there appeared the conveyances bearing the native ladies attached to the regiment. The question agitating the mind of Tommy Atkins was, would they or would they not get over? The ladies were seated in native carts called *ekkhas*, which carts were drawn by ponies; the carts had tops to them, and from these tops descended curtains which effectually hid the dusky beauties from the eye of any chance spectator. Just as the line of carts had safely passed the centre of the bridge, a cry was heard: "It is gone!" It was too true; the boats which had faithfully held together during the passage of Her Majesty's soldiers, the camels and the baggage, gave way under the immense responsibility now entrusted to them, and amid despairing cries, boats and *ekkhas* were borne away by the current of the swollen river. Which bank would they reach? The eddies of the river might carry the oar-less boats anywhere: they might be carried down to the Indus, they might be taken back to the bank from whence they started, but for once the treacherous eddies proved propitious; watched by anxious eyes, the boats bearing their precious burdens gradually but surely neared the shore, and as they touched, many willing hands caught and secured the wandering boats; the *ekkhas* were brought safely to land, and the ladies re-stored to their position with the regiment.

Five days later we were once again on the banks of the great Sutlej river. When we had last seen it on June 25, there were wide reaches of sand down to the stream itself; and it was spanned by a bridge of boats. Now the river was bank full, the bridge of boats gone, and we had to cross over in boats. It was raining heavily all day long, the tremendous current swept us all down, some boats going two to three miles down stream; some of our baggage was carried so far down that it was three days before we saw it again, and when we did get it every thing was soaked through. After crossing we marched to Loodiana, where we halted till August 3.

On August 11 we were within three marches of Delhi, and could hear the cannonading quite plainly. A day or two before, Nicholson had left us and had ridden on to Delhi to confer with General Wilson; the object of his visit to the camp was to advise that on the arrival of his force, the city should be assaulted immediately. Unfortunately this advice was not taken; had it been, we certainly should not have suffered as we did. The regiment was 680 strong; the men, all old soldiers, were seasoned by the marching we had gone through, for including halts, we had averaged eleven miles a day since we started.[1] We had with us one

[1]

		MILES
May	25, Left Sealkote.	
	26, Camp . .	15
	27, Wuzeerabad .	14
June	1, Moodkee Serai	19
	2, Anarkullee (Lahore) .	18
	10, Camp . .	19
June	11, Umritzur (halt 4 days) . .	17
	15, Jundiala . .	11
	17, Reyah . .	12
	18, Gorana (cross Beas) . .	9
	19, Kurtalpoor . .	10

wing of H.M.'s 61st, the 2nd Punjaub Infantry, the 4th Sikh Infantry, the 17th Light Field Battery, one wing of the 7th Punjaub Police Battalion, and last, but not least, the 250 Mooltanee Horse. No doubt the contest would have been severe, no doubt we should have lost

		MILES
June	20, Jullundur (halt 3 days) .	12
	24, Phugwarra . .	11
	25, Phillor (halt 3 days) . .	12
	30, Phugwarra . .	12
July	1, Jullundur .	11
	2, Kurtalpoor . .	12
	3, Gorana . .	10
	4, Reyah (cross Beas) . .	9
	5, Jundiala . .	12
	6, Umritzur (halt 4 days) . .	11
	11, Godaspore	42
	12, Trimmoo Ghaut and back	24
July	15, Trimmoo Ghaut	12
	17, Godaspore (halt 2 days).	12
	20, Camp . . .	10
	21, Buttala . .	10
	22, Camp . . .	11

		MILES
July	23, Umritzur .	11
	24, Jundiala . .	11
	25, Reyah . .	12
	26, Gorana (cross Beas) . .	9
	27, Kurtalpoor .	10
	28, Jullundur . .	12
	29, Phugwarra .	11
	30, Phillor . .	12
	31, Loodiana (cross Sutlej) . .	9
Aug.	3, Bara . . .	38
	4, Rajpoora .	19
	5, Umballa . .	15
	6, Shahbad . .	13
	7, Peeplee . .	13
	8, Kurnaul . .	19
	9, Paniput . .	18
	10, Sursowlee .	23
	12, Rhae . . .	12
	13, Alipore . .	10
	14, Delhi . . .	10

many men, but we were commanded by a man we knew and loved, whose presence was a tower of strength, and whom our men would have followed anywhere.

The month's delay in the camp before Delhi was most disastrous to us. On Sept. 6, only 20 days after our arrival, we had 340 men in hospital, chiefly with fever, and had buried many from cholera.

A letter written from Sursowlee, August 11, says: "I am pretty well, much better than I expected to be, but rather fagged with the marching; not getting a night in bed is hard work anytime, but worse here, as the days are too hot to sleep long or well. It is certain now we are not to attack Delhi by assault, but to wait for Sir Patrick Grant's force, which is coming up country."

CHAPTER V.

"His name was not stamped on those balls of lead."

VICTOR GALBRAITH.

ON August 14 we marched into camp; two or three bands came out to meet us and played us in. We brought down some siege guns, a quantity of military stores, and 9 lacs of rupees (£90,000).

As soon as we fell out I saw —— waiting for me, and he carried me off to breakfast with him; breakfast over, he proposed a ride round to show me the pickets, assuring me that the journey was perfectly safe. I soon noticed that the city seemed nearer, but my companion allayed all suspicion by telling me that there was a picket of our men in front at Metcalfe's house, whom we were *en route* to visit. Suddenly I heard the ping of a bullet, quickly followed by a second and a third, making the dust fly just before me on the road. I said, "Hulloa, what does this mean?"

"Oh, it is only the rifle-pits; we are just on their line of fire."

On hearing this, and seeing the picket just in front, I whipped up my steed and galloped into safety. When there, I turned round and saw my late companion, off his horse picking up my whip, which I had dropped, and then slowly remounting walk his horse into the picket. —— was one of those men who carried into practice the adage: "If I am going to be shot, I shall be shot." In the course of my life I have often heard men say this, though I have never met but three men who lived up to this fatalist doctrine. I well remember asking ——: "Were you ever afraid?" and his answer was, "Once. It was when we first came down here; I was General Barnard's orderly for the day, and I had fifty men of the 9th Lancers with me; when we came to the 'Ridge' we saw a lot of rebel cavalry on it, and I said to the General, 'I think, sir, I could clear that lot out. May I try?' He answered, 'You are a gallant fellow; go and try, by all means, but don't run too much risk.' Well, I started off, and the rebels, evidently not liking the look of us, bolted; we pursued them, when I suddenly saw them disappear behind a line of infantry who were drawn up just by Hindoo Rao's house; of course I was not going to stop for a lot of niggers, but for a moment I did think, Suppose the beggars stand? However, they broke and bolted, and we got back all right; but if they had stood it would have been nasty."

On another occasion we were together in one of the siege batteries; a live shell came in and began burying itself in the ground. Everybody except —— went down. I was face uppermost, and called out, "Lie down, you fool!" —— merely removed his cigar from his lips and said, "I am not going to put myself out for ——" The sentence was never finished, for at that moment the shell exploded, a fragment of it actually tearing off a piece of his trousers; he exultingly pointed this out in justification of the adage quoted above. Stories innumerable might be told of this man, whose experiences were not confined to India, and whose reckless daring is the subject of many a tale. The other man who lived up to this theory had had even a wider experience than ——. I well remember seeing him stand in the middle of a street, down which a heavy fire was pouring, calmly lighting a cigar. I was under shelter. I called out to him to come under cover; he looked up and said, "How often have I told you youngster that if I am to be shot I shall be shot, whether I am where I am or under cover?" and then, taking out another match, he proceeded to finish the lighting process which I had interrupted.

The third instance occurred on the day we assaulted Delhi; it took place at the Delhi Bank. The Bank house was surrounded by a large garden, and opened out on the Chandi Chouk, the principal street in Delhi, by means of a wide walled passage. The regiment was holding the passage, and a good many of us were in the garden behind the passage. The houses of the Chandi Chouk were thickly lined by the rebels, who kept up a constant and harassing fire upon us. Seated on the steps of the Bank was one of my greatest friends, a man I had known for many years. He did not belong to the regiment; he was sitting between two other men. I was standing near, but, owing to the passage, I was sheltered from the fire that came from the opposite houses, whereas they were directly exposed to it; they, however, had one advantage that I had not, a fairly comfortable seat. We had been talking for some time, when suddenly some bullets struck the masonry above where they were sitting. Hitherto the fire from the opposite houses had been directed on the men in the walled passage, but it was now evident that the Sepoys had perceived the men who were sitting on the steps of the Bank, and were directing their fire upon them. Seeing this, I urged my friend to change his exposed position, and come under the shelter of the wall. He replied with the saying already quoted. Hardly had he spoken when his two companions, one on each side of him, were simultaneously killed, one of them being struck by no less than seven bullets, the other with two; this was, of course, regarded by my friend as proof positive of the truth of his theory.

The picket I visited, as described above, was on our extreme left; it bore the name of Metcalfe's house picket, and had been the residence of Sir Theophilus Metcalfe during the time he was agent to the Governor-General of India at the Court of the Great Mogul.[1] Sir T. Met-

[1] He was also Deputy Commissioner of Delhi.

calfe accompanied the regiment to show us the way through the city on the day of the assault of Delhi. Twice I was privileged to hear him tell the story of his wonderful escape: the first time was at our mess-table, the second in a London drawing-room. The story was, that when the Mutiny broke out in Delhi, Sir T. Metcalfe stuck to his post until almost too late. It was not until the rebel cavalry were at the house that he escaped from a side door, and mounting his horse, which, owing to the forethought of his native servants, stood ready saddled, rode away to seek for safety.

His escape was at once perceived, and he was chased by the troopers. At first he gained upon them, but he soon discovered that his horse was not in good condition; he felt it was failing him, and he realised that unless events took some unexpected turn, he must be captured by his pursuers. At this juncture he saw a man on the road, and, pulling up, dismounted. He told the man that he was being pursued, and asked for a hiding-place, so that he could escape. Sir T. Metcalfe's own words, as well as I recollect them, were: "The man on this showed me a cave by the side of the road and told me to enter, saying he would save me if he could; he took my horse, and I went into the cave. It appears that he led the horse some little distance down the road, and then returned to near the entrance of the cave. My pursuers were not far behind, for I soon heard their horses coming along. Then I heard them interrogate my friend as to whether he had seen an Englishman on a horse go that way. He protested that he had seen no one.

They then went on, but soon returned, saying that they had found my horse, and consequently that I could not be far off. One of them must have noticed the entrance to the cave, for I heard him say, 'Perhaps he is in that cave.' My friend vehemently denied the possibility of this, and declared that for many hours he had been in his present position, and had seen no one. It was evident that they did not believe him, for I heard them say, 'At any rate, we will search it.' On this my friend burst out laughing, and raising his voice so that I must hear, he said, 'Oh, yes, search the cave; do search it, but I'll tell you what you will find. You will find a great red devil in there; he lives up at the end of the cave. You won't be able to see him, because the cave turns at the end, and the devil always stands just round the turn, and he has got a great long knife in his hand, and the moment your head appears round the corner he will slice it off, and then he will pull the body in to him and eat it. Go in, do go in; the poor devil is hungry. It is three weeks since he had anything to eat, and then it was only a goat; he loves men, does this red devil, and if you all go he will have such a meal.'

"I knew that I was intended to hear this, and to shape my action on what I had heard. I found that the cave turned at the end at right angles for a very short distance, leaving, however, plenty of room for a man to stand. Of course I knew how superstitious natives are, and how, above all things, they dread the unseen powers of darkness. I therefore drew my sword and waited. After more talking outside, my friend, who knew that the only way he could prevent them searching the cave was by frightening them, constantly urged them to go in and see the red devil. Some of them plucked up courage and entered. The cave was so narrow that they could only come up in single file. As soon as the first man came within my reach I struck at him with all my force. The blow fell straight, his head rolled from his body, and with a yell of terror, his companions fled out of the darkness. Lucky for me they did, for my sword had broken short off, and only the hilt remained in my hand. Mindful of my friend's warning, I lost no time in pulling the body of the fallen man into the recess. Their retreat out of the cave was the signal for a fresh outburst from my friend, who taunted them with: 'Go in, you will find Metcalfe there; if you don't, you will find the red devil.' 'Did you see him?' 'Isn't he beautiful?' 'Don't his eyes shine nice and red?' 'Do go back, he wants more than one; perhaps he has got two, for if Metcalfe went in he has eaten him.'

"But they had had enough; nothing would induce another man to enter. One of those who had fled declared that he had seen the red devil—probably to excuse the shame of his own flight, and this assertion finally decided the matter, and they rode away. When night had come my friend came to me, lodged me in his own house, and after some days announced to me that all was ready for my safe journey to Kurnaul. I left the man, assuring him of my gratitude, and telling him that when I had the opportunity that gratitude should be substantially expressed. When I took leave of my host, I asked him: 'Why did you save my life?'

"'Because you are a just and honest man.'

"'How do you know that I am a just and honest man? I have never seen you before this.'

"'Oh, yes, you have,' was the answer. 'You decided a case against me in your Court. I and all my family had fought that case through all the inferior Courts, and had won by lying, but you found us out; you saw we were lying, and you gave judgment against us. If you had given the case for me I would not have saved your life.'"

THE SUBZI MUNDI AND LITTLE MOSQUE PICKETS.

[To face p. 115.

CHAPTER VI.

> "Men will forget what we suffer and not what we do. We can fight.
> But to be soldier all day and be sentinel all thro' the night,
> Ever the mine and assault, our sallies, their lying alarms,
> Bugles and drums in the darkness, and shoutings and soundings to arms—
> Ever the labour of fifty that had to be done by five."
>
> DEFENCE OF LUCKNOW.

AT 4 A.M. on the morning of August 19 I went on picket to the Subzi-mundi; this was on the extreme right of our position and was garrisoned by a captain's picket of 100 men. The building we occupied was a native staging-house, a large square building with an imposing gateway, opening into a large square courtyard entirely surrounded by little archways, each archway being the entrance to a traveller's room, or to what we should call a hovel; the officers with the picket each had one of these, while the men were distributed in fours, two on duty, two in the hovel. The roof of these hovels was flat, and protection from the fire of the enemy was afforded by sand-bags placed along the top.

About 5 A.M., when on the top of the building, my attention was directed to three figures coming along the road from the city. I directed my glasses upon them, and soon saw that the two men and the boy were certainly not coming to us with any hostile intention, for they were unarmed, and they were hurrying along as fast as they could, constantly glancing backward, evidently fearful of something or some one behind them. I told the men not to fire upon them, and went down to the large gate that opened out on the road to await their arrival.

I had not long to wait before the three presented themselves for admission. I told the sentry to open the gate and let them in. No sooner was this done than the boy ran forward, and throwing his arms about my neck, kissed me, said something in English, and then burst into tears.

I at once took him to my quarters, and after a glass of brandy-and-water the mystery was explained. The boy was a woman; the sole survivor of the Delhi massacre. She had been saved by the chief Moulvie; had been in the city for three months and fifteen days, and had at last found the opportunity to escape disguised as an Afghan boy. She had to stay with us all day, as owing to the fire from the rifle-pits it was dangerous for any one to leave the picket in daylight.

As poor Mrs. Leeson grew calmer she told me some of the fearful sights she had witnessed in those awful days. She and some other women took refuge in a cellar; with them were a few men, notably a Baptist missionary. He had been my fellow-passenger on board ship—a very tall and apparently a very powerful man, a bloodless face, grey eyes, broad jaw, and a determined mouth. We youngsters used to try and get a rise out of him on board ship, but never succeeded, and as we thought him an awkward-looking customer we finally left him alone.

The men had managed to carry some provisions and ammunition into the cellar with them, and so provided they held at bay for some days the horde of desperate, murdering ruffians who attacked them. At last one by one the men fell, the ammunition was exhausted, the dead bodies of the fallen were piled up in front of the cellar as a breastwork, and behind that breastwork stood the missionary fighting for the women and children who were still alive with him in that pit.

For three days and three nights did this little band of men guard the women and children, never fainting, never fearing, always hoping for the succour that never came, until at last the missionary was left alone with nothing but his sword to protect his charge against the mutineers. Stripped to the waist, behind the ghastly rampart of dead the hero stood, and for hours this Horatius held his own. At last he fell, shot through the heart, and the blood-thirsty devils poured in. Mrs. Leeson was covered by some of the dead bodies which were thrown down as the mutineers rushed in, and so escaped the doom that was meted out to the survivors. As evening came on she crawled out of her hiding place;

she was at once seen and expected immediate death, but instead of death she found life, for the man who saw her, whether for past kindnesses or in hope of reward, told her to lie still till he brought her some things in which to disguise herself; this done he took her to the chief Moulvie's house, where she remained until she made her escape.

As she went along she saw the mute witnesses of those awful days, the dead bodies of English women who after unheard-of atrocities had been murdered and hung up on the trees in the city, the headless bodies of young children, and some men's bodies, the latter mutilated beyond all power of recognition. She told us that inside the city there was no alarm whatever on account of the siege; the defenders felt absolutely secure within their powerful fortifications. They were daily expecting that an outbreak of cholera or the advent of fresh mutineers on the scene, would compel the English to break up their camp and retreat to the Himalayas.

The news that an Englishwoman had escaped from Delhi was speedily sent up to camp, and about twelve o'clock Nicholson himself came down to the picket. He at once ordered the two Afghans to be brought before him; he received them in the middle of the square courtyard. He sat on his horse in the full blaze of the sun and earnestly regarded the two men; at last he spoke.

"You were tried at Peshawur three years ago and convicted of felony and sentenced to fourteen years' imprisonment."

The man looked up at Nicholson and then fell on his face, exclaiming—

"My Lord and my God!"

Nicholson then addressed the second man, detailing to him his crimes and the sentence he was under. He then prostrated himself. Then Nicholson told them to rise, and said to them, that as they had saved this woman's life and brought her in safety, their lives which were forfeit would be spared on condition that they acted faithfully. He then told them that they would be employed as spies, and said to them—

"Do you believe that if you are faithless to the trust, my arm is long enough to reach you wherever you are?"

The men, who were visibly trembling, declared that such was their faith. Once after this it fell to my lot to give one of these men the password in order that he might get safely back from the city.

On August 20 the cholera, which had been long foretold, burst upon us. Although cholera is almost unknown in the city of Delhi, its suburbs and the land beyond it are a yearly prey to this fell disease. The safeguard of the city is a ridge of low hills, which causes the miasma that rises from the marshes to be borne over the city. Our camp was pitched on the *marsh*[1] side of the ridge.

On the night of the 20th I had just come in from patrolling in front of the picket, when I heard a man cry out in pain. I at once summoned the apothecary who was with the picket, and we made the discovery that it was a case of cholera. Of course I reported the case to the Captain, and he took what steps he could to isolate the case, but it was useless. A few minutes more another cry told that another man had been

[1] The Nujufgurh swamp-drain ran just at the back of the camp.

seized, and from then the seizures went on with alarming rapidity; in half-an-hour more than half our picket was down, unfit for duty, and we sent up to camp, asking either to be relieved or reinforced.

Meanwhile the Captain, thinking that sometimes prevention was better than cure, took a dose of chalk mixture and opium, a favourite remedy in those days, and instructing me to call him at nine in the morning and visit the guards every hour, went to sleep.

At the appointed time I failed to wake my Captain, and everything being quiet, and feeling rather lonely, about ten I decided on visiting the next picket, where a brother ensign was, to have a chat. Soon after getting there we were joined by a third, who came in from his picket further on the left, and we three agreed that, if possible, we would all dine together that evening, for if we could manage such a dinner we could get a joint out from camp—a luxury on picket; but the possibility of such a feast hung on the slender thread of my Captain's slumbers. To my great delight, when my Captain awoke about twelve, he, after enquiries as to all being well, announced that he should take another dose, the sleeping effect of which would wear off about 9 or 10 P.M., when he said he would take the whole duty and send me to bed. As soon then as the fresh dose was safely down I ran across and gave the news, and the order for the dinner was at once despatched to camp. I stayed all day at that picket, for it was a wonderfully quiet day, no firing going on, and no excitement of any sort.

At seven we had our dinner, and about 8 P.M. we three were sitting outside under a verandah enjoying cigars and coffee, when on a sudden we heard a great shouting, accompanied by a heavy musketry fire, and almost immediately we heard our heavy guns from the batteries above us open fire. We all jumped up and separated. My road back was straight towards the city, and in consequence directly towards the disturbance. I ran along the road, and to my horror saw that there was an assault being made on the pickets, for I could see in front of me swarms of men running towards me, firing and shouting as they ran; it now became a question of speed as to which would get to the gate of the picket first. Of course the assaulters had not seen me, although I could see them. I ran at my top speed, and just got to the gate in time to get in and to get it safely shut before the rush of mutineers came alongside. My first visit was to my Captain's hovel, and much delighted was I when I saw him sleeping peacefully. The assault was soon over and no harm was done, and next morning at 4 A.M. we were relieved and marched back to camp.

The dreariest experience I had of picket work during our month before Delhi was one day when I was sent to the rear picket. In the early days of the siege this used to be a very important and at times a very lively berth, but as time went on the mutineers quite neglected this position, and when I was there it was deadly dull; the reason of stationing a picket there at all was to guard the dry bed of a nullah, a sort of very wide, deep ditch, up which a surprise party might come. In this ditch we had three sentries, one in front of another, and the only duty one had to do was to visit them.

The rear picket had no house, only a tent; there was an artillery officer on duty there with some guns that commanded the nullah, and he and I were the inhabitants of the tent. The place itself was the burying-ground of the animals that died in camp, and hither were drawn the dead bodies of the horses and camels. When I was there, there was in addition to these the huge carcase of an elephant. I called it the burying-ground, but the bodies were not buried; no earth was ever disturbed for them; they were drawn there, and left for the adjutants and the vultures, and they let us know, especially the elephant, that they were unburied.

Flies are always a nuisance in India, but on this picket they gathered together in special numbers. Our only amusement, and that soon palled, was tying together two large bones, and seeing two adjutants swallow one each, and have a tug of war as to which should get both bones. The last night I was on that picket I thought I was in for an adventure. I was visiting my sentries about twelve, and had passed two of them, and was looking out for the third man, the most distant one. Not hearing him challenge, I cocked my revolver, and advanced very quietly, expecting every moment either to see the sentry or some of the mutineers. At last the stillness was broken by a groan, and on going to the place I found my poor sentry down with cholera. I got him on my back, and carried him into our camp; but it was all over with him, and at 5 A.M. I buried him, with some others, in the men's burying-place. I often had to perform this office, for whenever I was in camp I was always willing to do it.

It may be a matter of surprise that in a camp in which there were two chaplains, an officer should bury instead of a clergyman. Of the two chaplains who were with the force, the senior, Mr. Rotton, had nothing to do with our part of the camp; his work lay elsewhere. The other chaplain died a year after in an up-country station of the very disease he so dreaded—cholera—an isolated case.

But although our men did not see much of the chaplain, they had a spiritual helper, an Italian priest, who came at his own expense from the Punjaub, and pitched his tent close to the hospital tents, so that he could be called on at any moment. He was always to be found in the hospital, or, when fighting was going on, in the field. His black dress, wide-brimmed hat, and gold crucifix, were always to be seen where duty and where the love for suffering and dying humanity called him.

When we left Delhi in October, and went into cantonments in the Punjaub, this Italian priest was at the same station. On Christmas Day that year my turn of duty took me to the Roman Catholic Chapel.

It is a custom with the Roman Catholics to subscribe a sum of money, the only salary he gets, for their priest at Christmas. In spite of protests from the Roman Catholics, the whole regiment had insisted on subscribing, for, they said, "He was the man who looked after us all when we were before Delhi, and we don't see why we shouldn't subscribe for him as well as you." The difference of opinion between the faithful and the grateful became so acute, that the attention of the officers was drawn to it, with the result that they all joined in with the men for the Christmas offering.

When the little priest had finished his sermon, he said: "Now, my friends, I have to thank you for the handsome Christmas-box you have given me; but it is not *you* who are here I want to thank, for you have but done your duty. But those others, those who do not belong to our faith, those are the ones I want to thank for their generosity to me."

So highly, indeed, did we esteem the little priest, that he dined at our mess an honoured guest—the first, and, I should imagine, the only instance of an Italian Jesuit priest dining at the mess-table of a Queen's regiment.

I saw a good deal of the good little man, and I once asked him how he could, in action, discriminate between the faithful and the heretic. His characteristic answer was: "Ah, my friend, in Rome the saints are good, and the Virgin Mary is very good; but here, where the cholera is doing its deadly work, and where the bullets are flying round, the saints are no good—the Blessed Virgin even is no good. All I do is: I hold this" (shewing his crucifix) "before the eyes of the dying man, and say, 'Look at the figure of Jesus! Jesus Christ died for you! Believe on Him, and you are saved.'"

The extreme terror which some men have of infection or contagion, is doubtless often the cause of the disease. A remarkable instance of this was afforded in the case of a man who was in hospital for a wound in his wrist. In the next cot to him was a man with cholera, and when I went round the hospital the man with the wounded wrist besought me to order his removal to another tent. Such an order was out of my power to give; however, I told the man that I would gallop back to camp, get the order, and be back within half an hour. Meanwhile I tried to calm his fears, and, to reassure him, I went to the cot of the cholera patient, who by this time was comatose, and put my face close down to the face of the dying man. There was no heroism in the act, for in those matters I am a confirmed fatalist, but I thought and hoped it would reassure the man, who was evidently much frightened. I galloped down to camp, got the order, was back within the half-hour, only to find the poor fellow in the last stage of cramps, and the deadly blue colour over his face.

Visiting the hospital entailed one very unpleasant as well as necessary duty. There was one small tent into which the men who had passed into the comatose state were placed just before they died; this tent had to be visited in its turn, and walked through from one end to the other; the usual question, "Any complaints?" had also to be asked. Of course no answer could be given, for the inmates of that tent were either already dead, or so close to death that there was no real difference.

On September 1, I had my first turn of Delhi fever; fortunately for me it was only a mild attack, and next day I was fit for picket work again. So notoriously unhealthy was the side of the Ridge where our camp was, that in the old days when cantonments were there, it was no uncommon occurrence for the Native Infantry regiments who tenanted them to have as many as 800 sick during the months of August and September. If the natives of the country suffered in this way, it is not surprising that the white troops felt the deadly effects of this most unhealthy spot. As it was, the excitement kept us up, with indeed the occasional change of air on picket duty, either at the top or on the other side of the Ridge.

On September 2 a brother officer and I determined that as we had been unable to keep St. Partridge's day as we were in camp, we would, at any rate, get something next morning. We had taken our shot guns with us on picket, and very early in the morning of September 3 we sallied out to try our luck. We were rewarded, for after several attempts we succeeded in bagging a fine peacock, a sitting shot in a tree. It is true that we had a novel experience, for while we were trying to bag our peacock, the rebels in the rifle pits were trying to bag us.

On September 4, the long expected siege train arrived, but even then it was not complete. When our column came down on August 14, we brought some siege guns with us, and these guns, with the new ones, had only now to be supplemented by some mortars for all to be ready to begin.

Monday evening, September 7, the trenches were opened; we were to advance our line of attack from 600 yards to 150 yards. At seven o'clock that evening, a party of the regiment, consisting of a captain, two subalterns, and 120 men, went up to the Engineers' Park, where we received pickaxes and shovels, and started on our errand. We had got down the road some little way in front of Metcalfe's house picket when we were halted; no one knew the way, and we had to send back for a guide. Hour after hour passed; we sat or lay down on the wet ground with nothing to do except to watch an occasional red-hot shot, far over our heads, fired from the city. It was 12.30 before we got down to our place; there we found the 1st Bengal Europeans and some of the 60th. We at once set to work, cutting down trees, filling sand-bags, digging out a trench; we worked as noiselessly as possible, all orders were given in a whisper, but in spite of every precaution we were heard, and about 2 A.M. a huge blazing "carcass" was dropped close to us. We all lay down and escaped unperceived; however, the defenders were not quite satisfied, and sent some rounds of grape which passed harmlessly over us. Just before daylight we retired, and the first night of the trenches was not attended by the loss of a single man.

On Thursday I was down in the trenches again. This time it was very different, everything was known, assaults on different points were frequent, and the fire was severe; still we had opened Ludlow Castle battery, and that kept our opponents fairly well employed. It was on this occasion that Eaton of the 60th had a marvellous escape. A piece from a bursting shell struck him on the back of the head, taking off a largish piece of his skull; we all thought he was done for, but he recovered and lived for many years after this with a silver plate on his head, on which, in addition to his crest, was engraved his monogram and the record of the wound.

The Mosque picket on the ridge was only a short walk from our quarters in camp. As from it we had a good view both of the city and of our batteries, we often used to go there, especially of an evening, to see what was going on. From the top of the Mosque the road to Delhi from the south was plainly to be seen, and over and over again we strained our eyes for the long expected cloud of dust heralding the approach of a force from the south. Our home letters told us how at the outset of the Mutiny, people in England did not realize the gravity of the situation; but as time went on, when the news of the Cawnpore massacre must have been known in England, we felt sure that troops would be sent to our assist-

THE MOSQUE.

[To face p. 140.

ance, and could not understand their non-arrival.

We little knew what difficulties the southern force would have to overcome, nor did we guess that they were expecting help from the north.

One evening, when I was up at the Mosque picket just at sunset, every gun on both sides opened fire; the effect was magnificent. At the same time, the mutineers began firing rockets which enhanced the beauty of the scene. While I was there, a round shot struck the Mosque high up; it passed through a room in which some of the men were playing cards, knocking down mortar, &c. on the table. The advent of that shot was followed by a speedy emptying of the room, and a sudden termination of the game of cards.

Enervating as the climate was—and

there is no heat so oppressive as the heat at the end of the rains, when the whole country is more like a huge steam bath than anything else—yet our spirits were not entirely damped, and we youngsters managed an occasional lark. One of these was at the expense of a subaltern who was shrewdly suspected of a lack of pluck. He had come off picket one day declaring that he was ill, and had gone to bed in his tent. There chanced to be a good deal of firing at the camp that day, and shells would sometimes burst over us. Sometimes, having lost their fuze, they would fall down harmless enough; one of these shells, known as "Whistling Jacks," from the noise they made passing through the air without a fuze, was secured by us. First we washed it out so that it was really harmless, then we got from the artillery lines a fuze, and having stuck the fuze in, we waited outside the tent of the sick (?) man. At last a shell burst over the camp; we lit the fuze and swinging the shell inside the purdah of the tent, called out, "Look out! shell in your tent!" The effect produced by this visitation was instantly manifested; the sick (?) man, who could not stand, ran out as strong as possible, to be greeted with the derisive cheers of the company outside.

CHAPTER VII.

> "The city's taken—only part by part—
> And death is drunk with gore; there's not a street
> Where fights not to the last some desperate heart
> For those for whom it soon shall cease to beat."
>
> Don Juan.

I CAME into camp very early on Sunday morning the 13th, so tired that I went to bed and missed thereby the early service, but I went to the mid-day one. Church was in a tent without any sides to it; two drums did duty for the altar, and the colours were spread over them for an altar-cloth. A great many attended both, officers and men; the latter all brought their rifles with them, laying them down by their side when they knelt down; the officers had their swords and their pistols in their belts. The service was the Communion Service. All was quiet until the

Consecration prayer. Hardly had the chaplain begun to read it when a shell burst over the tent in which we were kneeling; another and another in quick succession came hurtling through the air. Suddenly the first alarm bugle rang out; it was the signal for all to be prepared for an assault from the city; the firing increased, but still the priest continued reading, still the congregation knelt. At the moment when the officiating priest was partaking of the Sacrament himself, the second bugle was heard; every man sprang to his feet, arms that had been laid down were grasped, the tent was rapidly emptied, and every one was running as fast as his legs could carry him to his post. Our post was close by, so I soon reached it and heard the reason of our sudden summons. The rebels had come out of the city, and it seemed as if they intended under cover of their fire to make an attack on the camp. The fire from our guns soon changed their intentions, and they sought safety behind the walls of the city. Then we returned, and the service was finished without further interruption.

In the afternoon there was a Council of War; it was held in a tent pitched for the purpose, and was guarded from spies by sentries posted at a distance of 100 yards. The sentries kept meeting each other as they paced backwards and forwards. As the tent in which the Council was held had no sides, we, who stood beyond the sentries, could see the legs of those seated at the Council-table, and could also see right through the tent. I mention this to show how impossible it was for any one to have been concealed in that tent. This Council, we afterwards knew, settled the final plan of assault for next day, and arranged the details of the attack. Every one of the councillors—there were about ten of them—was pledged to absolute secrecy. The Council broke up a little after 4.30, and yet, when we took the Cashmere Gate next morning, an order-book, similar to the book then in use in the army, was found dated "Palace, September 13, 5 P.M.," giving the exact detail of the force that was to assault the Cashmere Gate, and sketching out generally and briefly the other points of attack of the other assaulting columns.

How was this news conveyed? It is impossible even to imagine that any one of the councillors had betrayed his trust, and had he done so, how could a messenger have passed from our camp into the besieged city? No one could have been concealed inside the tent, no one could have guessed where the tent would be pitched in which the Council was to be held; no carrier-pigeon could have carried a document so bulky as the full detail of the assault must have been. It remains one of those mysteries which some day may be easy of explanation, but which at present is insoluble.

Being far from well and very tired I turned into bed early that night, leaving untouched a glass containing castor-oil with drops of opium in it, prescribed for me by our regimental doctor. At 12 o'clock I was awakened by the Adjutant shaking me, and heard him say, "We parade at 2·30 for the assault at 3." The first thing I did was to swallow the stuff I had let alone before going to sleep, the next was to enter into a long and animated discussion with the sharer of the tent as to the clothes we should wear. Finally we decided that we would wear the best things we were possessed of; this resulted in his annexing one of two flannel shirts I had been carefully treasuring for future use. He promised a return of the shirt, but this promise was never performed, for he was wounded, slightly it is true, but the bullet so tore the shirt that he preserved it as a memorial. Then we put all our things in order in case of anything happening.

My companion had a long struggle with an arrangement he had designed to enable him to fire a double-barrelled pistol with a stock to it with one hand; that took some time. At last, however, it was declared perfect. So it was in theory, but when he tried to put the theory into practice the result was disastrous, for he shot one of our own men through the foot, and had to pay compensation to the man for the accident.

Of course, after the announcement we had received, sleep was out of the question, so when all our arrangements were completed we started out to find our friends and see what they were doing. Gradually, however, we gravitated toward the mess-tent, where we filled up our bottles and whiled away the time before parade as cheerily as we could. The "bottles" were due to the forethought of our Colonel; they were soda-water bottles covered with leather and slung round the neck with a strap which passed under the sword-belt. Not only had all the officers one of these bottles, but all the men had one as well. When therefore the allowance of rum was served out—that morning the allowance was doubled—our men put the rum into their bottles, and did not, like some others, drink it off sooner than leave it.

We paraded for the assault under the command of our Major,[1] a soldier of a bygone type, an Irishman, a good rider, a capital judge of a horse and of a good bottle of wine, beloved in the regiment by officers and men. His *forte*, however, was not commanding a regiment. His first order to move out of camp was so curiously worded and so scrupulously obeyed, that the result was the hopeless "clubbing" of the regiment; seeing the dilemma the Major turned to one of the Captains with "——, like a good fellow, get them right;" but the position was now such that even science could not successfully alter it; whereupon the Major with great readiness gave the

[1] Our Colonel was in command of the column, consequently the command of the regiment devolved upon the next senior officer.

order "Halt," and then, "Fifty-second, get yourselves as straight as ye can," an order that was cheerfully and laughingly obeyed.

At 3 A.M., in the darkness of night, we started. We had got about a mile and a-half on our journey when we were called to a halt; something had gone wrong, no one of us knew exactly what it was, but we stopped for an hour and a half, losing the precious darkness, and watching the daylight creep up into the sky. Many of our men fell out here, some indeed had fallen out at the start—men whose bodies had been weakened by fever, but whose courage induced them to try to be sharers in the assault on the city we had been outside of so long. While we halted, Nicholson passed by us; his last words were, "Good-bye! I wish I was going with you."

At last we drew up close to Ludlow Castle; it was daylight now. As we stood on the road a shrapnel shell came just over my head and burst behind me, killing two men and wounding seven more; singularly enough, another which soon followed, and which burst apparently in the same place, touched no one.

While we waited, the 60th Rifles passed by in skirmishing order; they were going to try and clear the walls, which we could see were densely covered with mutineers; they could not do much, for they were exposed, whilst their opponents were shielded by the battlements. Soon we saw their wounded being carried by us, not much of an encouragement to our men, who well knew what lay before them. Here we were joined by the Engineer party who were to blow open the Cashmere Gate; one of these, Salkeld, was an old schoolfellow of mine. We had not seen each other since we had left school, and were mutually surprised to meet where we did.

When we advanced down the road for the assault, he and I walked together till within about twenty yards of the glacis, when he went on to do his duty, and to die a hero's death. For a minute or so we stood on the road, then a storm of fire rained round us and the order was given to lie down; this was promptly obeyed—indeed one of ours obeyed the order so promptly, that not looking for his resting-place, he threw himself into some cactus-bushes that grew just the other side of the road, the sharp thorns of which made their existence suddenly and painfully perceptible.

Most of us took refuge in a wide but shallow ditch that ran alongside of the road. From this partially sheltered position we saw a storm of bullets pour down upon the road on which we had just been standing, and tear up the dust in all directions. One of the ladder-party, who immediately followed us, finding that his comrade had dropped his end of the ladder and sought safety in the ditch, remained on the road with the end of the ladder still on his shoulder. His Captain called out to him, "Come under cover!" He lustily shouted for some one to come and help him with the ladder, but this idea of duty cost him his life, for he fell dead almost immediately, pierced by many bullets. So heavy was this fire, directed at us from a distance of only about fifty yards, that a Crimean veteran who was present said that even in the Crimea he had never seen anything to exceed it. As we lay in the ditch, our eyes were naturally directed to the place where we knew the gate was. Suddenly we saw a column of smoke rise up, then we heard, indistinctly it is true, but yet audibly, the bugle ring out the "Advance." At the sight of the smoke most of us had jumped to our feet. Away we went. Inside that sheltering glacis was security from the murderous fire to which we had been exposed. As I ran I saw Captain Bayley on the ground. For a moment I stopped—"Shall I pull you under cover?"

"No, go on."

I saw my Captain, Crosse, go in through the hole in the gate, it was only large enough to admit one at a time. I was going next when Corporal Taylor pushed me on one side and got second; I came next—third man in. Through the gateway we saw an open square, the sunlight pouring into it—empty. Under the arch of the gateway stood a nine-pounder gun, loaded actually to the muzzle. I put my hand in and drew out a bag of nails, bits of iron, &c. Near to and around the gun lay some dead bodies, the defenders of the gate, the men who had shot the devoted Salkeld as he nailed the powder-bag on the gate; though riddled with bullets, he handed the fuse to fire the train, which blew up at the same moment the gate and the defenders of it.[1] The gate was soon thrown open, and our men, Coke's Rifles and the Kumaon Battalion, who formed our assaulting column, poured in after us. The whole column formed up in the large open space inside the gate-

[1] The story that a naked white man was attached to this gun is as devoid of foundation as another tale, that a naked white man was fastened to the Cashmere Gate.

way, and while there we saw the column which had been told off to storm the Cashmere breach, come over the walls. Our Sikhs had fired a *feu de joie* in the air just before the arrival of the stormers. While waiting in the square, one of my brother officers addressed me with—"Halloa! you are wounded; blood is running down your leg." It was not the case, but I found I had had a very narrow escape; the soda-water bottle covered with leather, which in common with the rest I carried, and which my sword-belt held down over the hip, was broken by a bullet which, tearing my trouser, passed between my hip and the bottle. Part, however, of the liquor was still in the bottle, and my companion proposed that we should at once share what was left, promising me a share out of his bottle later on. I was not thirsty,

THE BREACH AND CASHMERE GATE.

[*To face p.* 158.

so he took it all; but when the time came to claim repayment, my friend's bottle was empty.

We soon moved on, guided by Sir Theophilus Metcalfe, and came to the entrance of the Water Bastion; as this was one of the places assaulted, it did not seem worth while stopping to enter; however, we went in and found it full of the enemy. They were so astonished by our appearing in their rear, that they hardly showed fight, but fled panic-stricken to the walls to scramble or jump down. One of ours, a big fellow he was, cut at one of the mutineers as he was escaping, and with his sword—only a tailor's one—all but cut his head clean off.

Later on that day a brother ensign and myself had an opportunity of testing our swords. We attacked a man, not both together, but one at a time. I had the first try, and my sword bent almost double against the man's chest without inflicting any wound. My companion fared but little better, for his sword glanced along a rib, inflicting a long, shallow skin wound, and had not the revolver been handy, it might have been awkward for one or both of us. From the Water Bastion we turned into the city in order to get to the great Mosque, the Jumma Musjid, which was our destination. As we turned we lost some of our men, who, with their officers and the Kumaon Battalion, went in a different direction. As we passed along the streets we noticed large basins full of different sorts of liquor, put out by the natives, who had full knowledge of the British soldier's drinking propensities. We heard afterwards that this liquor was all poisoned. As we went along we broke these basins and spilt the liquor. When close up to the Bank we met the first sign of opposition, a howitzer with some men round it. Unwilling to lose men, our Colonel ordered us to halt, and, taking a few men, he made a detour so as to get behind the gun and its guardians. Unfortunately, our Major, who was left in command, mistook the Colonel's orders, and before the latter could get round, ordered a charge. The gun was taken, but we lost one of our officers, who was shot dead, and several men. Nothing more occurred on our forward journey, and we arrived at the Jumma Musjid only to find its great gate closed and the houses round it filled with numbers of the enemy, who kept up a hot fire upon us. We drew a little way back, so as not to be exposed to a direct fire, and then waited for the other columns which never came. Our numbers were seriously reduced: the Kumaon Battalion had vanished, most of Coke's Rifles were also gone, some fifty of our own men had gone the wrong way—all told we could not have been more than 150 strong. Our Colonel, however, would not retire; he said, "The 52nd have never retired without orders yet, and as long as I live they never shall," a speech loudly cheered by the men who heard it. Meanwhile, as we waited, the Ghazis made some desperate charges upon us. They came galloping down the street, their linen clothes flying in the wind, their tulwars waving round their heads, shouting "*Deen, Deen, Allah Deen!*" straight on the points of the bayonets. None ever went back, they came to die, and die they did, but every time they came, some one of us was killed or wounded.

The day was wearing on, some news had reached us through some Sikhs who came to us; they told us that with the exception of the assault on the Cashmere Gate, all the others had failed, and that Nicholson was killed.[1] At last the order to retire came—we were to fall back on the church. By this time, however, we were surrounded, and to get back appeared hopeless. All the officers shook hands with one another and said "Good-bye." Our dead we had to leave, our wounded we took with us; we got some native beds and some shutters to carry them on, and putting them in the middle we started. Very different was that retreat to the advance. As we came up

[1] General Nicholson was not killed on the 14th, but was mortally wounded; he died on the 22nd.

hardly a shot was fired, now the houses on each side seemed alive with men, and cavalry kept on charging down the street as we retired. A brother ensign and myself were with the rear guard; we used to halt some of our men, make them kneel down in the street, fire, and then we ran on to overtake the rest of the rear guard. As the regiment came out on the broad Chandi Chouk, a very wide street with a walled canal in the middle of it, which we had to cross at right angles, the Sepoys who were in front attempted to close the gate at the end of our street. This was, however, prevented. When my companion and I got to the entrance, we, who were the last to go, discussed whether we should go straight across, climbing the low wall of the canal, or whether we should run up the street until we came to a bridge crossing. We did not know that there was a bridge immediately in front of us, and we could not see for the smoke that was hanging about; we decided on going up the street, and accordingly we started as hard as we could run.

The attack on the Lahore Gate having failed, the mutineers had flocked into the Chandi Chouk, and had got guns there with cavalry and infantry. As we two boys ran up the street searching for our bridge crossing, we ran straight towards a large body of men who were in the street, and our men who had got over were astounded at the sight they saw. They saw us two running headlong at a large number of men; suddenly they saw these men turn round and run also. They evidently thought that we were the *avant couriers* of a charge of infantry. The clouds of smoke which had hidden the bridge crossing from our view hid what was behind us; for all they knew hundreds might have been following—at any rate they were not going to wait to see, and bolted incontinently and so saved us. Then the spectators saw us turn over the bridge crossing and come back, but we were not fated to continue the impressions we had first made; some of the rebel cavalry saw that there were only two of us, and made a dash to cut us off. Just as they were on us, we swerved close to the canal, where some small trees were growing, and as we came opposite to where our men were, they came out into the street, and we crawled in somehow under the horses of the enemy, unharmed and unscathed.

At the Begum's Bagh, where we now were, we were rejoined by our missing men, and by the Kumaon battalion. For some time we stayed where we were, losing more men than we lost at any other place, for we were exposed to a direct fire from the houses opposite, and could not retaliate. At last, however, we left it, and got back to the church, which was close to the Cashmere Gate, about 11.30 o'clock.

As we had been without food since dinner the night before, our thoughts naturally turned to what was to be got. We were much rejoiced by finding our mess-servants with plenty to eat and drink; we were more thirsty than hungry, and my companion and I at once set to work to quench our thirst. I had a bottle of soda-water in one hand, and a long tumbler in the other, into which tumbler my companion poured some brandy. His allowance, however, was so generous, that I dreaded drinking it, especially on an empty stomach, and I told him not to drink it either. Not liking to waste it, we looked around us, and saw a group of officers on the steps of the church, apparently engaged in an animated conversation. Among them was an old man, who looked as if a good "peg"—the common term for a brandy and soda—would do him good. Drawing, therefore, nearer the group, in order to offer the "peg" to the old officer, we heard our Colonel say: "All I can say is that I won't retire, but will hold the walls with my regiment." I then offered our "peg" to the old officer, whom we afterwards knew to be General Wilson; he accepted it, drank it off, and a few minutes after we heard him say: "You are quite right—to retire would be to court disaster; we will stay where we are."

On such little matters great events often depend; for if the English troops had left Delhi, in all probability there would not have been one of us left to tell the tale.

Just as my companion and I had comfortably settled down to some cold mutton and claret, we were ordered off to the College to relieve the 61st; we had to leave our dinner and go. When we got there, we sent out a strong picket to occupy an archway which commanded one of the towers of the magazine. Some two hours after, I was sent out to relieve this picket, but I only had sixteen men with me, and some Ghoorkhas. I found that the first picket had been driven out of their position into some houses, and the officer I relieved told me that I should not be there very long, as the mutineers were gathering for an assault upon it. With the few men I had, I could see that I had no chance of holding the houses, so I begged him to get reinforcements sent out. Soon after he left, the heavy fire drove us back from our house into one behind. Two of my men were shot, four were badly wounded, my Ghoorkhas ran away, and when the real attack came I only had ten men. Seeing that matters were hopeless, I told the ten men to go back in single file, and waited.[1] As they came on I fired my revolver into them, and then walked out—I thought it useless to run. I did not see how I could escape, for, besides the fire behind

[1] One of the survivors of that sixteen told me how well he remembered it all, and that he used to tell how, when he was in that house, and had been firing away until "he was black in the face," he sat down for a moment to rest; that "the young officer who had lately joined the regiment, said to him 'Make haste and rest, they will be on us directly' The 'Make haste and rest,' always amused him."

me, I had to pass for 100 yards in front of the magazine wall at a distance of thirty yards. I measured these distances afterwards. The wall of the magazine was crowded, and the bullets cut the ground up all round me. However, I escaped untouched, and right glad I was to find myself once more in safety behind the College wall.

At 4 P.M. we were relieved, and went back to the church, where we finished our interrupted dinner, and then, tired out with thirteen hours of excitement and running about, I searched for and found some empty sand-bags, and carrying them into the church made up a bed, and went to sleep for some two hours. I was awakened by some one rudely shaking me; I opened my eyes, and saw a live shell blazing away on the floor of the church. The mutineers were shelling the church; all the other occupants had been aroused by the bursting of the shells, and had got out, and our Adjutant came in to get me out also. I was soon sound asleep again outside.

So ended from my point of view the assault of Delhi. The loss of the assaulting force was very heavy. My regiment lost ninety-five men and five officers killed and wounded,—just one in every two; for though we were returned at 240, only about 200 took part in the assault. The loss in the whole force was over one in four, for though the assaulting columns were nominally composed of a thousand men, making a total of 4,000, the actual number engaged was nearer 3,700 than 4,000. The official return of the whole force was 66 officers and 1,104 men killed and wounded. From what we saw afterwards, we judged that the loss of the defenders of the city was less than ours.

Our loss would have been much heavier if we had had to encounter the full force of Sepoys who had flocked to Delhi, but numbers, which have been variously computed at 10,000 up to 40,000, like the Assyrians of old, "heard a rumour," and marched out of the city on Sunday night —some never to return again.

CHAPTER VIII.

> "North, was the garden where Nicholson slept;
> South, was the sweep of a battered wall."
>
> SIR ALFRED LYALL.

BEFORE continuing the story of the street-fighting inside the city, the account of the adventures of a private soldier of the regiment who took part in the assault may be given. There was a man in the regiment of the name of Peter Dignum; he was an unlimited service man, who had been fifteen years in the regiment, and for many years past had been annually tried by regimental court-martial for habitual drunkenness, and as regularly sentenced to twenty-five lashes with the cat. Now when the Mutiny broke out, Peter did not relish the idea of a hot-weather march, so one fine night, when Peter was posted as sentry, he decamped with a native lady from the bazaar, and the pair retired to the lady's village, where Peter enjoyed idleness amid the cooling breezes of the hills.

But lotos eating is expensive, and so when Peter's available cash was run short, and food was no longer to be obtained, he retraced his steps, and gave himself up as a deserter, and was, in the ordinary course of events, forwarded to his regiment to be tried by a general court-martial for desertion. Consequently Peter came down country in a bullock-cart, with two white bullocks and a guard. The Government carried him comfortably along the road down which his comrades in arms had marched, carrying their kit, and thoughtfully provided a guard in order that Peter might not be lonely in his long journey. On

Saturday, September 12, he arrived in the camp before Delhi. On Sunday General Wilson promulgated an order that all or any prisoner for military offences might volunteer for the assault. Peter volunteered. On the way down to the assault, Peter was taken so unwell that he had to fall out and return to hospital. The exact nature of his disease was so recondite, that it baffled the skill of the doctors to exactly diagnose it.

When Delhi was finally taken, General Wilson declared an amnesty for all those prisoners who had taken part in the assault—Peter, of course, included; but benefits did not stop here. In addition to a free pardon, Peter, as having taken part in the assault, became entitled to six months' extra pay, and a share of the Delhi prize-money. But from that hour he became a marked man, for whom retribution was waiting. Had he not malingered on the day of the assault he might—nay, probably would—have got off scot-free. But that malingering was a crime his comrades would not, could not pardon. At last the day came—once more Peter yielded to his old temptation, and again appeared before a regimental court-martial, charged with habitual drunkenness; this time the full penalty for the offence was meted out to him, and he was sentenced to fifty lashes. As a general rule, the men hate seeing a comrade tied up to the triangles to be flogged. In this instance, however, the exception which proves all rules was found, and expressions of delight were numerous that the malingerer was to be flogged. Heartily were the lashes laid on, twenty-five by a right-handed bugler, and twenty-five by a left-handed one. When the punishment was over, Peter put his jacket on and fell into the ranks.

Much as the short-service system has been condemned by soldiers, no one will deny that in the old long-service system there were many old soldiers who were as clever shirkers of their duty as Peter Dignum.

At four in the morning of the 15th, after a hasty cup of tea, I was sent out to relieve one of our fellows on picket. I found the place was close to where I had been driven from on the previous day. On my right, and communicating with me, was a very strong picket of the 60th Rifles, some cavalry, and some artillery-men with guns. Soon after getting settled, I noticed that the Sepoys were threatening to assault our side of the picket. I got as many of the 60th as

I could, and was joined by some of the artillerymen. These, with the fifty men I had, made up quite a strong force, and filled up the house we were in as full as it could hold. When we were once packed we had not long to wait; the Sepoys came on at us in a dense mass. We gave them a volley at about twenty yards, and then charged out upon them; they fled in every direction. We chased them through the houses out of which we had been driven the day before, and right up to the gates of the magazine. We brought back with us the bodies of the two dead men I had left. They were horribly mutilated; every conceivable indignity had been heaped on these mute witnesses of the fiendish barbarity of the savages with whom we had to deal. About 10 o'clock the rest of the regiment came up from the church, and I was at once detached with my fifty men to another picket.

To give the detail of each of the day's street fighting in Delhi would only weary the reader; there was a sameness about them, yet every day was full of incidents.

One day, about luncheon time, several of us were in a house, which we had got into by knocking holes through the walls of other houses. This mode of progression was rendered necessary because the Sepoys occupied houses which commanded the streets, and to attack them directly would have entailed a constant loss of life, and this we could not afford.

The question was raised as to who should get some food. At last it was decided to draw lots as to who should run down the street and get some food from the mess. The lot fell on one of the Captains. He got down all safely, and we saw him coming back with something in his hand; when he caught sight of us he raised what he was holding over his head and waved it. Suddenly we saw it struck out of his hand and fall in the street. He picked it up, but when he arrived we found that the cold leg of mutton he was bringing had a bullet through it.

Of course at times we had to cross the street. On one of these occasions a man was wounded; he cried out for water, and a water-carrier who was with us, went to him, and from his *mussuk* was giving him water. The Sepoys fired on him, a bullet struck the *mussuk*, and the water spurted out. The gallant fellow took hold of the *mussuk* with his disengaged hand, stopping the flow of the water; another moment, and another bullet came, this one hitting the poor water-carrier and killing him.

Sometimes we got into the basement of the houses before the Sepoys had time to escape. Generally they were in some large room on the first floor. Up we used to go, batter in the door, throw ourselves flat on our faces for the volley which always came when the door was open, and then rush in, and make short work of those inside. One time, as soon as the door fell, no volley came. I looked up, and saw instead of armed mutineers a quantity of beds ranged along the wall like a hospital. A rapid inspection showed that they were tenanted by women. I called out to the men:

"Turn out, we will go up stairs; they (the Sepoys) must be on the upper floor."

Some of the men had followed me into

the room; I was just going out and was standing by the doorway. All the men but one were out, when to my horror I saw the man who was still in the room raise his firelock and bring it down with violence upon the bed. At once I ran to the man, threatening him with dire punishment for being such a coward as to hurt a woman, when the man, an Irishman, said—

"Och, yer honour, did ye iver see a woman with such a prutty moustache as this?" and raised from the bed the unmistakeable face of a Sepoy.

To recall the men was only the matter of a moment, and ordering the girls all to get up—it was during the daytime and they were all dressed—we found the firing party we were in search of, who having heard us come in through the wall, sought for safety under the bodies of the women.

The man who made the discovery explained afterwards, that although the order had been given not to hurt the women, no order had been given against kissing them, and he had merely placed his arm round the girl's neck to give her a kiss, when he became aware that his hand in its passage round the neck of the girl had come in contact with the face of the man underneath.

A somewhat similar case to the above occurred a day or two after, when an order came from head-quarters to pass some women down the street. The veiled procession was moving down in single file, when one of the sentries, by whom each had to pass, lifted a veil and saw a man's face; after this the other officer who was present and I, posted ourselves in the street and compelled each woman to lift her veil before we allowed her to go by. By adopting this course we stopped a considerable number of Sepoys from escaping, as all who were discovered were immediately executed. Of what was going on in the other parts of the city we at the time knew very little, but in our part, during those six days of street-fighting, only once did the fighting differ from guerilla warfare—the exception was in the struggle for the possession of the Bank. This building was in a large garden close to the Chandi Chouk, the main thoroughfare of Delhi. Three times did we and the 60th Rifles assault it; three times were we driven out of it, and it was only on the fourth attempt that we succeeded in holding it.

Our method of attack was, first, men with their bayonets cleared the building itself, then others followed, carrying sand-bags which were placed in front, then the men lay down behind the sand-bags, firing. But the Sepoys had a nine-pounder gun in the Begum's Bagh with which they used to clear us out with rounds of grape. At last, however, sand-bags enough were added to shield us from the grape, and then we soon cleared away the gunners from the gun. Just as all was over, our sand-bags well up, men firing through the loopholes, I was standing looking through a loophole at the now fast retreating Sepoys, when young ——, who had just got his commission in the 60th—he had been in the East India Company's service—pulled me away, saying, "Let me have a look!" and fell back almost in my arms, shot by a random bullet through his right eye. Poor fellow! he lived two or three days, but never recovered consciousness.

THE DELHI BANK.

[*To face p.* 185.

Some of our men were posted on the top of the Bank, where, partially sheltered by the balustrades, they kept up a fire on the houses opposite. Among them was a private named Knight,[1] who had been reported killed on the day of the assault; as a dead man he was not entitled to either rations or grog, and for two days had maintained a precarious existence. He told me that he saw Sergeant Jones, who with one exception was the tallest man in the regiment, but whose courage was not in proportion to his inches, come up on the top of the Bank to serve out some grog to the men, who were in dire need of food and drink. As soon as the Sergeant appeared with the grog-can, a bullet ricochetted from the balustrade and struck the can; down went the long

[1] There were certainly three men of this name in the regiment, and there may have been more.

Sergeant flat on his face, dropping the can, out of which the grog began to flow. The men on seeing this called out, "For God's sake, Sergeant, don't spill the grog; never mind yourself!"—a remark that was hailed by a burst of laughter, which increased as the Sergeant, on hands and knees, crept round to serve out each man's allowance.

While this street-fighting was going on, our quarters, especially the sleeping ones, were very uncomfortable. Tuesday night another officer and I shared a wretched little room in which there were three dead Sepoys. We dared not sleep out of doors, for in the street in which we were posted the Sepoys had a nine-pounder gun, which gun they used to run round a corner in the street with a slow match in it; its charge of grape duly fired, they pulled it back by means of a rope to reload. The next evening we took that gun, and then moved our beds out of doors. Even this position was perilous, for no night passed without one, or generally two, charges from the Ghazis. Our orders not to seek to engage in the streets were so peremptory that when our Colonel appeared next morning on his usual visit, I had considerable misgivings as to how he would regard the capture of the gun. Looking at it he said—

"What is that?"

"Please, sir, it's a nine-pounder."

"Who did it belong to?"

"Her Majesty, sir."[1]

"How did you get it?"

"It came down the street."

"Lose any men?"

"No, sir."

[1] One of the guns captured in the city by the mutineers.

"Humph! don't do it again."

I was much relieved, as during the night awful visions of courts-martial had occurred to my mind.

One Sepoy contrived for a long time to be a source of great annoyance. He was on the ground floor of a house some way up the street, and used, after loading in security, to pop his head out of the window and fire; to hit him was an impossibility. At last we got rid of him. A Ghoorkha stole up the street on hands and knees, and got safely under the window. Out came the man's head, down came the Ghoorkha's *khookeree*,[1] and the Sepoy's head rolled into the street!

The stench from the dead became almost intolerable. Many of the men

[1] The Ghoorkha knife; this is such a powerful weapon that a skilful man can, with one blow, sever a bullock's head from its body.

could not eat their allowance of food. Heartily did I envy one of my brother officers who said to me, "What a dood ding it is to have a bad dold!"

Our constant advance through the houses prevented our servants getting to us with any change of clothes; as to washing, that was out of the question. The night-time was almost worse than the day. The men had to lie down in the streets. The heat was so stifling that they could not stand the houses; they put their rifles beside them when they lay down. On one picket they piled their arms in the street; but on a false alarm—and these were constant, principally on account of the number of drunken men about—the piled arms were knocked over, and several rifles broken by the fall. Sometimes the alarms were real; one night I woke up, heard shouting and firing, and saw a blazing port-fire just being put to the gun under the muzzle of which I was sleeping.

The picket[1] I had the command of was almost the centre of the line of advance, which, on account of its semi-circular form, diverted the out-going traffic down our street. No one was allowed to carry off any plunder; all was to be reserved for the prize-agents. Among the many things we got and handed over were the gold *lotas* from the Palace; these, placed in pyramid form, made quite a show.

In our street were the principal liquor stores of the city; over these we had a special guard to prevent any one entering, while inside we had natives breaking the bottles of wine and spirits day and night. No one could stand the fumes long, and

[1] This picket consisted of 50 men of the 60th Rifles with their own officer, and 50 men of the 52nd.

the breaking-party had to be constantly relieved. One day a ruffian from another regiment shot our Corporal, who was guarding the entrance, and rushed down the steps into the cellar. He was soon arrested, and as we had no place suitable for keeping a man in custody, especially such a violent culprit as this—for the man was quite half-drunk when he was arrested—we tied him up to a post, in the shade, until we could hand him over to the proper authorities. The head-quarters of the army were in Skinner's house; this was in the same street as our picket.

A considerable number of officers from native regiments that had been disarmed or mutinied, hung about head-quarters; and some of these men, in spite of all that had happened, were still so infatuated with the idea that their adored

Sepoy had only been led astray by a few evil men, and that the mass were still loyal and only wanted an opportunity to return to their allegiance, that they were very indignant with my fellow commander and myself because we immediately executed all the male prisoners we got. There really was nothing else to be done, except to let them go free, and this, with the Cawnpore massacre fresh in our minds, was out of the question. These unattached officers became such a nuisance with their everlasting protestations that we had to put sentries on to keep them back. One of them all but succeeded in releasing a prisoner. He came to us and told us that he had been talking to the captive, and the man had assured him that he had joined his fellows much against his will; that when they mutinied he had saved the life of one of the officers of the regiment; that he loved the English, and that he was rejoiced at having got back to the white faces again. The officer who told us all this, vouched for the sincerity of the tale, and in consequence we told the man to stand out; hardly had this been done, when a young officer came up and asked us if that man was pardoned. On being told, "Yes," he said, "He was a trooper in my regiment. I know he killed one of our officers with his own hand, for I saw him do it, just before I escaped myself."

Late on Thursday evening, a native brought me a verbal order to rejoin the regiment with the men who were with me. Not feeling absolutely certain whether the order was genuine or not, I walked behind the guide with my pistol close to his head, assuring him that on the slightest symptom of his leading us into a trap, he would be the first man shot. It was pitch dark at the time; the man led us by crooked streets and tortuous ways safely to the gate of the Magazine where the regiment was.

In the Magazine our quarters were very comfortable; we, the officers, were lodged in a long, large room; at one end was our mess table, made of boxes and shutters, above it a circular bayonet-stand bristling with bayonets. The firing from the Selimghur fort still went on; every now and then a round shot would strike our building. Many speculations were indulged in as to what would happen should a round shot strike the bayonet-stand while we were round the mess table. On Saturday night the long expected actually happened; we were all in bed at the time; a round shot came in, hitting the bayonet-stand plumb in the centre;

the effect on the bayonets was not to scatter them in all directions, but to merely dislodge a few of them and to break down the stand.

On Friday morning I got my first wash since Sunday; there were no tubs to be got, so we took turn to squat down and have a *mussuk* of water poured over us. Enjoyable as the water was, the operation was not unattended by danger, for we were plainly seen by the rebels opposite us, who could not deny themselves the pleasure of firing at us during our ablutions; they never got nearer hurting anyone except with pieces of plaster from the walls which they dislodged. Never indeed was the cleansing of our bodies more necessary; since Sunday morning none of us had had a chance of washing anything except face and hands; we had not been able to change our clothes;

some of us, owing to the beastly quarters and the filthy *charpoys*[1] we had had to lie upon, were covered with vermin.

Just outside the magazine house the artillery men had fixed some mortars, with which they shelled the still defended parts of the city. Being very anxious to try my hand with a mortar, I persuaded the officer in charge to let me regulate the charge of powder in one of the mortars. My great desire was to get a shell inside the Jumma Musjid, that great Mosque outside of which we were stopped on the day of the assault. At last, some one found the right elevation and the correct charge, then we sent shell after shell into the great Mosque, but we were soon stopped. A messenger from Col. Baird Smith came galloping up with, "What are you doing? Stop that instantly!" We

[1] Native bedsteads.

THE JUMMA MUSJID.

[*To face p.* 198.

were then told that we were not to fire on the Mosque or on the bridge of boats which we could see on our left. At the time we could not comprehend the latter part of this order, but next day, when we saw the bridge crowded for hours together with people leaving the city, we realised the full significance of the command.

The authorities were glad to get possession of the city, and did not wish to shut up the Sepoys who were still in it, like rats in a trap. As to the great Mosque, our shells did little harm; when all was over, I went to see the Mosque, and found that our shells had only cracked the pavement where they fell, and not injured the architecture of the beautiful building.

Saturday evening found me on picket again; this time just outside the Palace. Early on Sunday morning the 60th came through the picket, and after blowing open the great gate of the Palace rushed in. I went in with them; there was no opposition, the Palace was deserted, and we roamed at will through the different rooms. Facing the square was a beautiful hall, open throughout, the further side looking over the river, the descent from the hall to the river being almost precipitous. The walls were marble inlaid with cornelians of various colours, representing the petals of flowers; the centre of these petals had been precious stones, but these were all gone before we got in. With the taking of the Palace the siege of Delhi ended, the strong fortress which our engineers had made was fallen, the King of Delhi was a fugitive, to be brought back a captive a few days later by Hodson, and the backbone of the Mutiny was broken. The issues that hung trembling in the balance

THE KING'S PALACE.

[To face p. 200.

on the success or failure of that assault were momentous. It is an open secret that Sir John Lawrence wrote to Nicholson, that if Delhi did not fall by the 20th of September, he could not hold the Punjaub after that date.

It is futile to speculate on the "might have beens." Delhi had fallen on the 20th, and the Punjaub was safe. The leaders of men in the Punjaub and in the north-west accepted Sir John Lawrence's assurances, but not so the people. Even when the Mooltanee Horse laden with plunder marched back through the Punjaub, the people who saw them said, "The English have given them this plunder to make us believe that Delhi is taken." It was not until the 52nd returned to the Punjaub that the people really believed that the city they imagined to be impregnable had fallen, for they recognised us, and felt assured that if Delhi had not fallen, we should not have been alive to come back.

But what of Nicholson? On the day of the assault he was wounded in the covered way between the Lahore and Cabul Gates, whence he was carried to the hospital tent, and by a coincidence laid beside his brother Charles, who was also wounded. He was seen by Doctors Hare and Broome, who, after examination, told him that his wound was a mortal one. From the hospital tent he was soon removed into another, pitched on purpose for him. In deference to a request, Dr. O'Callaghan, who was in charge of the artillery, came to see him. He confirmed the report of the other doctors, and taking Nicholson's hand in both his own, pressed it, and left the tent unable to control his feelings.

The men of the Mooltanee Horse

gathered round that tent; their anxiety to have the earliest news of how their great chief progressed would brook no delay; they wanted to see with their own eyes, and hear with their own ears. Anyone who came out of that tent was eagerly questioned for the latest news, but silent watching was as irksome to them as it is to all natives, and soon the buzz of their conversation as to whether the Sirkar[1] would fail, whether the Sahibs would all be killed, varied by that topic of never failing interest to the people of Hindustan, *annas* and *pice*, penetrated through the canvas of the tent and reached Nicholson's ears. He sent for one of them, and told him that the talk annoyed him, that he was very ill, that he needed rest, and ordered silence to be observed. For some twenty minutes

[1] Government.

all was quiet, then the conversation began again. Ill and dying though Nicholson was, he would make them understand that no man should disobey him with impunity, so taking a pistol from a small table by his bedside, he fired it through the tent walls. The bullet hit no one, but the exclamation, "*Wah, Wah, Generale Sahib ke hookhum hai*,"[1] showed the lesson had been learnt, and the conversation ceased.

Nicholson was not disturbed at the prospect of death, but he deeply regretted that he was not to live until the work on which he had set his heart had been accomplished. It had long been arranged that after Delhi had fallen, a force of which he was to have had the command should march to the relief of Agra, and then proceed down the Grand Trunk

[1] "Oh! oh! there is the General's order!"

Road to effect a junction with the Commander-in-Chief. Nicholson had often talked over his plans, and to one of his intimate friends he had said jokingly, "I am certain that old —— Colin will put me under arrest before I have been twenty-four hours with him."

In his illness he took a very gloomy view of the future; he feared lest another might fail[1] where he felt confident of success, and he said, "If ordained to fail, I hope the British will drag down with them in flames and blood, as many of the Queen's enemies as possible."

During the month we were besieging Delhi, Nicholson held no official command;[2] high qualifications and undoubted

[1] Malleson's "History of the Mutiny" shows how nearly failure occurred.

[2] The one exception was soon after our arrival at Delhi, a hostile force left that city to intercept the siege-train coming from Ferozepore, which, in consequence of the withdrawal of troops from the Punjaub, was only

merit had to give way to seniority of service. Although he was no longer in command, our men did not recognise the altered conditions—to them he was, *par excellence*, "the General." I well remember an occasion when Nicholson on his rounds, not on duty, passed one of our men, who, after saluting him, said—

"Jack, here's the General, present arms."[1]

Nicholson acknowledged the salute, and said—

"Thank you, but I am not *General*, only Captain Nicholson."

To a man whose ready determination and force of character impressed all with

slenderly guarded; Nicholson, in command of an expeditionary force from camp, encountered the rebels at Nujufgurh, and entirely routed them.

[1] A sentry would "present" arms to a General; to any other officer he would only "carry."

whom he was brought into contact, to have to serve under General Wilson, whose vacillating conduct at the time of the Meerut outbreak entailed the sacrifice of thousands of lives, must indeed have been gall and wormwood. For looking back on those days, no one can doubt that if a man of Nicholson's stamp had been at Meerut, English soldiers would never have felt their cheeks crimson and their hearts burn at the news that rebels, numerically inferior to English troops, could in the face of those troops march triumphantly from the scene of their rebellion, with their drums beating and their colours flying, to spread disaster and to seize the stronghold of Northern India. Indeed it may be true that Nicholson, after he received his mortal wound, when he was told that General Wilson thought of retiring from Delhi, exclaimed, "Thank God, I have strength yet to shoot him if necessary."[1]

On the day of the assault, Nicholson was entrusted with two points of attack. First the breach by the Cashmere Gate, and second the advance along the walls to the Lahore Gate. Certainly, no one knew the way along those walls better than John Nicholson, for while we were besieging the city, this wonderful man, in his usual dress, with no attempt at disguise, passed along those very walls, through the batteries—going indeed in an opposite direction, namely, from the Lahore Gate to the Cashmere Gate. This sounds like romance, and it may well be asked how a man like John Nicholson, with his strongly-marked personality, could have passed along the walls and through the batteries of the

[1] Holmes' "History of India," p. 398.

besieged city and come out alive to tell the tale. No one but he could have accomplished this act of seemingly reckless daring, and even for him the risk was tremendous. That night his star was in the ascendant, and on his way he met no Sepoy. The batteries were manned by Sikh gunners, detained in the city against their will by the mutinous Sepoys, who prostrated themselves in reverence when they saw the giant figure of the man they believed to be their Incarnate God.

The Cashmere breach he also knew, for on Sunday night, September 13, accompanied by his Brigade-Major, impatient of the delay, and desirous of adding his personal testimony to the fact that the breach was practicable, he saw with his own eyes that it was possible to carry the breach by escalade.

Two days after the Palace fell, John Nicholson breathed his last; the indomitable will of the man who had declared that he would not die till Delhi had fallen, had kept him alive till the work for which he had given his life was virtually accomplished. At last the weary days and nights were ended, and the most distinguished soldier of those who saved India for the English was at rest.

Verily it was the case with John Nicholson that, when the time comes, the man is there; no other could have done what he did. True, that he had exceptional opportunities; equally true that he made a marvellous use of those opportunities. Colonel Malleson, in his admirable "History of the Mutiny," thus speaks of Nicholson: "He died with the reputation of being the most successful administrator, the greatest soldier, and the most perfect master of men in India. The reputation was, I believe, deserved."[1]

On Wednesday evening, September 23, it was known that Nicholson was to be buried on Thursday morning. As usual, the remnants of the regiment went through a sort of formal parade just outside the magazine building in which we were housed. Parade was over, Colonel Campbell was just moving off, when a private[2] stepped out of the ranks with: "If you please, Colonel, the men want to know if they are going to the General's funeral to-morrow."

"Certainly not; the regiment will parade at the usual time to-morrow morning."

As the parade was always held just after daybreak, no one could have been

[1] Malleson's Indian Mutiny, p. 310.

[2] When parade is dismissed any soldier may speak to the Colonel, but in doing this he must be attended by a non-commissioned officer.

present at the funeral who had to be on parade. Then the old soldier spoke again, and said: "Colonel Campbell, I joined the regiment before you did, and you know the character I have had while in the regiment. I mean no disrespect, sir, but *we are going*."

Campbell flushed up, and replied angrily: "The regiment shall not go; if necessary, I will use force to stop them!"

"And what force will you get, sir? The regiment will march through all the other regiments that are here."

Campbell was wise enough to see the spirit that was abroad, and turned away as if he had not heard the last remark, the end of which, however, must have pleased him.

This was the sole instance of insubordination I ever saw in the regiment. During all those days of street fighting, although liquor of all sorts was abundant, no man of the regiment was ever drunk, or even the worse for drink; and the order not to plunder, but to give up to the prize agents all that was found, was so strictly adhered to, that a month or so afterwards, I, amongst others who were desirous of having something for a memento of Delhi, offered to purchase from the men anything they might have kept, and found that so rigidly had the order been obeyed that nothing was to be had. The men of the 52nd in 1857 thus showed themselves worthy successors of their Peninsular predecessors, for it was always a legend in the regiment that when, after the battle of Vittoria in 1813, the French treasure chests were upset, and the gold pieces scattered on the ground, the 52nd marched by that gold without a man falling out of the ranks for plunder.

Early on Thursday morning the regiment, with but few exceptions, marched out of Delhi to John Nicholson's grave, just outside the Cashmere Gate. No one who stood by the open grave that September morning could fail to be affected by the impressive scene. The body was borne on a gun-carriage in dead silence. No band played the Dead March; no volleys of musketry were fired over the great General. Chief amongst the mourners stood Neville Chamberlain, his devoted friend; and surrounding the open grave were officers and men, some with sunburnt faces, some bleached white by fever and sickness, their plain *kharkee* uniforms contrasting with the picturesque dresses of Pathans and Afghans, and others of his Mooltanee Horse. The solemn words of the beautiful burial service, read by the senior chaplain,

Mr. Rotton, were accompanied by deep sobs from those who stood round, for not a dry eye was to be seen.

But the most remarkable part of this scene was after the coffin had been lowered into the ground; then the men of the Mooltanee Horse gave way. Throwing themselves on the ground, they sobbed and wept as if their very hearts were breaking; and be it remembered that these men held the creed, that a man who shed tears was only fit to be whipped out of his village by the women. Probably not one of these men had ever shed a tear; but for them Nicholson was everything. For him they had left their frontier homes, for him they had forsaken their beloved hills to come down to the detested plains; they acknowledged none but him, they served none but him, they obeyed none but him. They believed as others, that the bullet was not cast, the sword not ground, that could hurt him; over and over again in the frontier skirmishes had they seen Nicholson pass unharmed where others must have been killed; and now that the earth was placed on his coffin, they threw their traditions of manhood to the winds, and over John Nicholson's grave poured out the flood of their pent-back love.

These men never took any pay whatever for their services, and when, a few days after Nicholson's funeral, an order was received by them from head-quarters to march somewhere—I do not know where—they returned for answer that they owed no allegiance to the English Government; that they had come down to protect and serve Nicholson and to loot Delhi; both of which they did to the best of their ability. And when they had

NICHOLSON'S GRAVE.

[*To face p.* 217.

collected as much plunder as they could, they marched back again, up country, to their own homes, carrying their plunder with them.

In 1866, nine years after the Mutiny, I stood one early morning by John Nicholson's grave. Careful hands had tended the resting-place of this English hero. The inscription on the gravestone placed by General Neville Chamberlain is:—

THE GRAVE
OF
BRIGADIER-GENERAL
JOHN NICHOLSON,
WHO
LED THE ASSAULT OF DELHI,
BUT FELL
IN THE HOUR OF VICTORY
MORTALLY WOUNDED,
AND DIED,
22ND SEPTEMBER,
AGED 35.

CHAPTER IX.

> "Unthread the rude eye of rebellion,
> And welcome home again discarded faith."
>
> KING JOHN, Act. V.

It may be urged that in those days unnecessary severity was exercised towards the mutineers, but it must be remembered that it was no civilized war we were engaged in, no quarter was ever asked for, even had it been it would never have been given; we had to deal with a race whose interpretation of the word mercy is "the fear that kills." Years after the Mutiny, in a shooting expedition in the Himalayas, I came across some of the Sepoys who had escaped. In conversation with them, I said, "If Lord Dalhousie had been Governor-General, would the Mutiny have broken out?"

The man to whom the question was addressed turned as pale as his brown skin would allow, and, visibly trembling even at that distance of time, at the thought of what would inevitably have happened, answered, "God forbid! he would have swept us off the face of the earth."

Another instance may be quoted illustrating the method which natives themselves employed to stamp out mutiny. Horrible as the cruelty was, yet the awful sufferings of one man probably, nay certainly, saved thousands of lives and untold misery. At the very time that our Mutiny broke out, a rebellion took place in the Cashmere territory. Gholab Singh, whose treachery to his people had been rewarded by the gift of the fair valley of Cashmere, had died, leaving as his successor Rhumbeer Singh. One of his brothers, whether his step-brother or own brother, I know not, raised the standard of rebellion and claimed the throne. He received considerable support, and matters looked bad for Rhumbeer, but the latter, by prompt action, secured the person of his brother, summoned all the chiefs, disaffected and loyal, to Jummoo, where he tried the aspirant to the throne for rebellion. He was found guilty, and punishment decreed. The culprit was led out in the presence of all, he was suspended by the hair from an overhanging beam, and then was lowered one inch into a caldron of boiling oil. Next day the same process was repeated, and so on day by day until exhausted nature gave way under the torture, and the unfortunate man was released by death from his sufferings. It was reported that Rhumbeer then said,

"Anyone found in rebellion against me will be severely punished, and not treated to the merciful death given to my brother." The rebellion was thus stamped out.

Our life in the Magazine was by no means an unpleasant one. It was something after all those weeks of tent life, to have a good solid roof over one's head, something that really did keep off the rays of the sun. Every day we had a charming breeze from the river, our appetites were good, food was now plentiful, and health and strength began to come back. Our make-shift table was soon replaced by a real table at which we could sit in comfort, and we were no longer alarmed by the bristling trophy of bayonets at one end of our mess-table. Many of our fellows were invalided to the hills; they had held on to the last in order to be in at the taking of Delhi. Monson[1] held on almost too long; he had been ordered away some time before the assault, but he would not go; he came off the sick list to take his turn of duty, but had to go on again directly. At last he was so ill that he was sent off, whether he liked or not; it was just before the assault. He got on all right till about thirty miles from Simla, when he fainted, and when he arrived at Simla, the doctor there thought the bearers of the *palki* had brought him a corpse, and told them so; however, he pulled round, and was ultimately restored to health.

One of our fellows arrived at the Magazine one day in high spirits.

"What is it?"

"I am going home."

[1] Captain the Hon. D. J. Monson.

"Home?" we said. "Why, what is the matter with you?"

He looked the picture of health.

"I am invalided; wait and I'll tell you all about it. You remember when I went out of Delhi ill?"

We did; and some of us remembered it only too well. The occasion was that one night he awoke dreaming that the enemy were upon him; he seized the sword that was by his bed—it was a cavalry sword he had got, having lost his own—and uttering a real Irish yell, began hewing his colour-sergeant who was nearest to him. The row that ensued was heard by some of the adjacent pickets, and we were awakened, thinking that an attack was on us. For this he was sent out of Delhi, sick. A medical board had been appointed soon after the capture of Delhi to enquire into cases for invaliding, either to the hills or home. Now for the story.

"I came up to the tent where the Board was sitting and just peeped in, and saw three old gentlemen sitting at the end of a long table; then I drew my head back. 'Come in, sir,' says one of them, so I put my head just inside the *purdah* and gave them a look. 'Come in,' they said, so I walked in very slowly, crouching down, with my eye fixed on the old fellow in the middle. I saw they were getting frightened, so I gave a little run and a real good Irish yell. Up they got and fled. I jumped on the table and made a terrific row, then I went out, and they have signed my papers for home, because I am mad!!"

He never rejoined us, but exchanged before his sick leave was up.

The 52nd was told off for the column

that under Sir Hope Grant was to march down country to Lucknow, but if they could not muster 200 men fit for duty then they were not to go. All of us were most anxious to go down, and great were the exertions made for the inspection. We did manage to get nearly 200 men out that morning, but when the inspection was over we were woefully short of the number; so many men had fallen out sick, even on parade, that it was apparent we could not muster the required 200.

At 3 A.M. on October 5 we left Delhi to march back to the Punjaub. It was a handful that came back: eleven officers, two doctors, and 160 men. This return to the Punjaub was perhaps the hardest of all the hard tasks of that year. The excitement was all over; there was nothing to be looked forward to, the long night hours of the regular march were never enlivened with a song—even the well-known "Jolly Shilling" was never heard. No band to play us out of camp, no bugle-band to take up the music—in fact our bugle-band was a thing of the past, and it was two years before we had the bugles to play at mess again. The men were jaded and weary, they dragged along the road, and we all felt a sense of relief when on the 1st of November we marched into Jullundur, where we remained until next year, when we got back to Sealkote.

I cannot close this brief account of the part taken by the 52nd Light Infantry in the great Mutiny better than by giving our Colonel's regimental order, dated October 5, 1857:—

"He cannot allow this opportunity to pass without expressing his thanks to the regiment generally, for the support he has received from all ranks in maintaining its reputation during the eventful period of the past five months. The regiment has always kept inviolate its very high name for discipline and good spirit; but a period of forty-two years had elapsed without an opportunity having been afforded by which it could prove the inestimable value of these good qualities when brought into play upon the field of battle. At the siege and assault of Delhi, the conduct of the regiment has fully realised the most ardent expectations of its commanding officer, and it is with the greatest joy and pride that he thus testifies to its admirable behaviour. Regularity in quarters has prevailed under great temptations; cheerfulness in the performance of arduous duties on picket and in the trenches; and at the assault of the city, its gallantry and devotion carried everything before it on its advance. Although he has noticed first the more brilliant part of the services of the regiment, the Colonel does not forget the praiseworthy conduct of the regiment during its harassing marches and counter marches through the Punjaub, as well as its conduct in the encounter with the Sealkote mutineers; nor can he forget to mourn the loss of the many brave and good soldiers who have fallen in the performance of these duties."

In 1860 Lord Clyde, as Commander-in-Chief in India, inspected the regiment at Sealkote. In addition to the usual march past, the regiment had on that occasion marched past in line, a most difficult manœuvre. The regiment was then formed into hollow square, and Lord Clyde, his voice frequently broken with emotion, thus addressed them :—

"Fifty-second! 'Tis now some fifty-three summers ago, when, a boy fresh from school, I found myself in action for the first time under the command of one whose name is familiar to the ears of the gallant regiment now before me—General Sir John Moore. You were then held up as a pattern to the British army, and in you I now recognize the same soldier-like bearing and discipline for which you were then so much and justly praised. You were always a gallant regiment, and it has always been your fate to uphold the honour of your Queen and country in whatever position you have been placed. To-day I watched with a scrutinizing eye your marching past, and cannot too highly compliment you. Every head was to the front, and not an eye turned to the right or left. You marched with a steadiness and precision not to be surpassed.

"Fifty-second! 'Tis now many years since I have had the pleasure of seeing you, but I recognize the same regiment with new faces. You have to-day realized the golden opinions of the olden time, and likewise the good opinion of all who see you, or under whom you serve, with credit to yourselves, and success to the arms of your country. I wish I had seen more of you, but I am confidently assured that your movements in the field would please me as well as what I have now witnessed. As I march to-morrow morning, I shall say, Good bye, and God bless you all!"

INDEX.

BRADBURY, AGNEW, & CO. LD., PRINTERS, WHITEFRIARS.